US INFANTRY - VIETNAM

squadron/signal publications

Near the Cambodian border, a LRRP scans the jungle for enemy activity. He is wearing the late war four color camouflage uniform, and has camouflaged his face with removable pigments.

A member of the 198th Infantry Brigade, Americal Division, rests during an operation near Chui Lai, in April, 1970. Many soldiers used their sox and locally purchased bags to carry additional rations and personal items.

Members of the 25th Infantry Division stand guard on the outskirts of a Cambodian village during the 1970 Invasion. The mixture of uniforms varied from unit to unit depending on the attitude of the commander.

An RTO from the 60th Infantry, 9th Infantry Division, in the Mekong Delta near the village of Moi Cai, fall, 1969. Plastic bag on phone is to keep moisture out.

US INFANTRY - VIETNAM

by Jim Mesko
illustrated by Amy Harroff

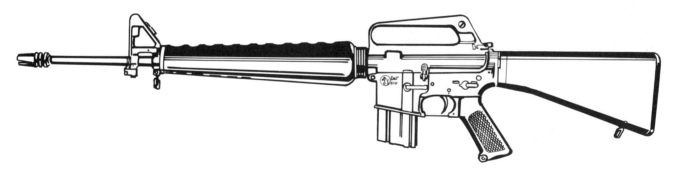

 squadron/signal publications

A machinegunner from the 25th Infantry Division fires on a Viet Cong position during operation CEDAR FALLS in January 1967. He still wears the early style combat boots and fatigues rather than the later issue jungle boots and jungle fatigues.

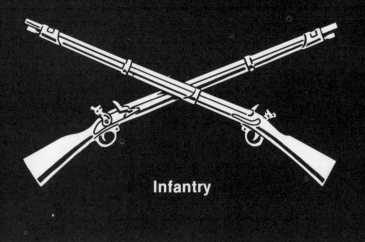

Infantry

If you have any photographs of the aircraft, armor, soldiers or ships of any nation, particularly wartime snapshots, why not share them with us and help make Squadron/Signal's books all the more interesting and complete in the future. Any photograph sent to us will be copied and the original returned. The donor will be fully credited for any photos used. Please send them to: Squadron/Signal Publications, Inc., 1115 Crowley Dr., Carrollton, TX 75011-5010.

DEDICATION

To all of the men and women who served in Vietnam, but especially to the "Grunts" who bore the brunt of the fighting.

PHOTO CREDITS

Peter and Stella Mesko
Pat and Louise Morris
Robert Seitz
Andy Chernak
199th Infantry Brigade, 12th Infantry, 4th Battalion,
    Company C
Dave Haugh
Rick Laney
U.S. Army
U.S. Air Force

The grim horror of war. Two men from the 173rd Airborne Brigade await a helicopter to carry the body of a comrade from the battlefield. (US Army)

INTRODUCTION

The first U.S. casualty in Vietnam was an army colonel who died in an ambush in Saigon during September of 1945. The last US servicemen to die in Vietnam were two U.S. marines who lost their lives in a rocket attack near Tan Son Nhut airport in April of 1975. During the intervening thirty years, approximately 56,000 Americans died in this worn torn land, with the bulk of these casualties occurring between the years 1962 and 1971. The majority of these US servicemen died, not in the sophisticated jet aircraft over North Vietnam, nor on the vast array of sophisticated ships in the Tonkin Gulf, but slugging it out in a vicious no quarter guerrilla war waged in the hot steaming countryside of South Vietnam. They fought against an enemy equipped with weapons ranging from primitive punji stakes to large caliber artillery. The enemy included the North Vietnamese Army (NVA), the indigenous Viet Cong (VC), and innocent looking civilians (men, women *and* children). The US Soldiers who fought this brutal war were mostly eighteen and nineteen year old draftees, often just out of high school. They were the infantry, the *Queen of Battle*. However, few, if any of these soldiers felt any glamour in slogging through the thick, insect ridden jungles or snake infested swamps, in their pursuit of an elusive foe. They soon coined a new word in the military dictionary, GRUNT, which they took as their badge of courage. And despite all the new technology introduced during the conflict, Vietnam was the infantryman's war. What follows is the story of the men who really fought the war in Vietnam, the infantry.

Terrain And Weather Conditions

A particular problem which faced U.S. commanders was the widely diverse terrain and weather conditions in Vietnam. Basically the country is divided into five major geographic regions each of which dictated certain tactics within that area. Following the dictates of these geographical areas the country was divided into military districts or Corps.

IV Corps

In the extreme south the Mekong Delta was crisscrossed by an extensive series of rivers and canals which watered numerous rice paddies and swamps. Even during the dry season the area was ill-suited for armored vehicles or motor transport, and during the monsoon season movement was nearly impossible. This area encompassed most of IV Corps and was the chief food production center of the country and contained most of the country's population.

III Corps

North-west of the Mekong Delta was a piedmont region which occupied III Corps. This piedmont was characterized by gently rolling hills and broad plains with lush vegetation. This made the terrain well suited for mechanized units, and throughout the war tanks and APCs played a prominent part in the war effort there. Within the boundaries of III Corps were located the infamous jungle bases of the Iron Triangle, War Zone C and D, and the major infiltration routes from Viet Cong sanctuaries in Cambodia.

II Corps

As Vietnam turns northward the terrain changes from rolling piedmont to the rugged central highlands. Numerous mountain ranges, cut by steep river valleys, are typical and are covered with dense forests. Few roads exist in this area and most troop and supply movements were by air. Tracked vehicle movement was extremely limited and the use of helicopters was greatly restricted because of a lack of landing zones (LZs). If conditions were not bad enough, inclement weather and dense fog further hampered operations. The only break in this rugged terrain was a rolling plateau on the western fringes of the highlands toward the Cambodian-Loatian Border. These geographic features made up most of II Corps, although there were a few areas of coastal lowlands at the foot of these hills.

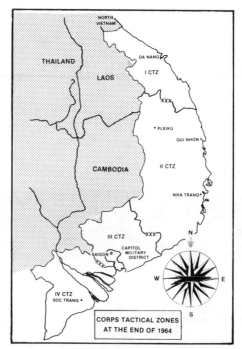

TYPES OF TERRAIN
SOUTH VIETNAM

☐ Delta
▨ Piedmont
◪ Highlands
▦ Coastal Lowlands
▨ Plateau

CORPS TACTICAL ZONES
AT THE END OF 1964

An innocent looking farmer tills his rice paddy in Vietnam. However, when darkness fell this same farmer often turned into a Viet Cong guerrilla, carrying out attacks on ARVN and US positions. (US Army)

4

I Corps

Coastal lowlands or plains were characteristic of the northeastern half of I Corps and extended roughly the entire length of this region to the Demilitarized Zone (DMZ), the border with North Vietnam. The main geographic features of the I Corps area were sandy beaches, wide flat river valley, marshes, rice paddies, and rolling countryside. Because of these conditions, this area was the second most populated area of Vietnam and the source of numerous commercial centers and agriculture production. This coastal plain extended only a short distance inland before meeting the rugged highland terrain which continued north from II Corps. The population was dense and severely hampered the use of supporting fire during operations.

Since Vietnam was located just north of the equator, between 8 and 17 degrees north latitude, the climate was tropical. Throughout the year the temperature was uniformly hot with varying degrees of humidity and rainfall. During the summer months the area from the piedmont, south experienced the torrential rains of the monsoon season with rainfall of nearly 80 inches. North of the piedmont in the highlands and coastal plains the monsoons came in the winter, with an average of over 100 inches of rainfall. The humidity rotted clothing, rusted equipment, and caused tremendous personal discomfort. On the other end were hot temperatures often in excess of 100°, clear skies, and little rainfall or humidity. Because of these climatic differences, the level of operations throughout the country varied from area to area during the seasons and made coordinated planning difficult across geographic and corps boundaries.

The Early Years

The first Americans to become involved in Vietnam were members of the Office of Strategic Services (OSS), the forerunner of the C.I.A. This came about toward the end of World War II when the OSS began helping the various guerrilla groups fighting the Japanese in Indochina. The major group involved in this struggle was the Viet Minh, led by Ho Chi Minh, an avowed communist. With the end of the war the French moved to reassert control over their colony. Other countries, including the U.S., dispatched military personnel to help in reoccupying the area and pave the way for a smooth transition of power between the Japanese, French, and nationalist forces. Under such circumstances trouble was an almost certainty, and as the various groups came into contact, fighting erupted. The Americans were caught in the middle of this political struggle but tried to remain neutral. However, after an OSS colonel was killed in an ambush in September 1945 near Saigon, they realized that there was little they could do to prevent full scale fighting between French forces and the Viet Minh especially since neither side was willing to make concessions. With in a few months this became a reality as the Viet Minh carried out a series of attacks against the French. A cease fire of sorts followed but in November of 1946 the war began in earnest and dragged on until the French were finally defeated in the climactic battle at Dien Bien Phu in May of 1954.

During the French-Indochina War the main assistance the United States provided was military aid although on occasion technical advisors and mechanics were temporarily stationed in Vietnam to train French personnel in the use of American equipment. Just prior to the fall of Dien Bien Phu, a group of air force mechanics were sent to help the overworked French ground crews as they struggled to keep the small French air force in operation against the Viet Minh. But the Eisenhower administration steadfastly refused to commit U.S. ground forces to the war in order to turn the tide against the communists. It was felt that any such effort would turn into both a political and military disaster. Thus the French cause was doomed, and following the fall of Dien Bien Phu, a ceasefire was agreed to and the eventual withdrawal of all French forces from Indochina.

The Geneva Accord, signed on July 21st, 1954, called for a temporary partition of Vietnam pending reunification by means of a national election. This election never took place. The pro-Western leader of the south, Ngo Diem, with U.S. support, proclaimed the Republic of South Vietnam. Diem felt that the communists would never allow *free* elections. Official recognition by the United States soon followed, and with this came military and economic aid. As the French advisors to the Army of the Republic of Vietnam (ARVN) withdrew, American personnel began replacing them until over 300 were in-country by the late 1950s. This American advisory force under designation Military Assistance Advisors Group (MAAG) had the responsibility for the training of the South Vietnamese Army and distribution of all military aid. The communists realizing that their chances for uniting Vietnam under Ho Chi Minh by means of the election were lost, turned to guerrilla warfare in an attempt to undermine Diem. As part of their plan, US installations and personnel were singled out for special attention. The first American casualties were two military advisors who were killed in a terrorist raid on Bien Hoa air base in the spring of 1959. As additional attacks occurred, ARVN forces, trained in conventional tactics, proved unable to counter the elusive guerrillas. Additional advisors were brought in during 1960, raising the strength of MAAG to 685 men, but even this had little effect on the overall war effort.

In January of 1961, the newly elected US President, John F Kennedy took office and in one of his first major foreign policy decisions, he approved a new counterinsurgency plan for Vietnam. This called for additional advisors and equipment along with some support and aviation units to help improve ARVN mobility. In December two helicopter companies arrived in country to carry South Vietnamese troops into combat against the North Vietnamese and Viet Cong. Following close on the heels of these units were elements of the 5th Special Forces Group, the famous "Green Berets" who were assigned to train various jungle and hill tribes in the art of modern warfare. With this influx of advisors and support personnel it was only to be expected that sooner or later they would become involved in clashes with the communists. By the beginning of 1962 the number of U.S. troops in Vietnam had risen to over 3000, yet even this substantial increase failed to help the South Vietnamese counter the growing strength of the guerrillas. More troops were sent in, and by the end of 1962 there were 11,000 US personnel stationed throughout Vietnam. Some progress was made in countering the enemy but widespread corruption in the Diem government negated advances on the battlefield. Dissatisfied with Diem, the Vietnamese army overthrew his regime in October 1963*, and set up a series of sort-lived civilian and military governments. In the face of the expanding war this government accomplished little, even with the doubling of U.S. personnel. By the middle of 1964 over 180 Americans had been killed while nearly 1000 had suffered wounds, along with 55,000 South Vietnamese casualties. In August of 1964, the North Vietnamese attacked U.S. destroyers in international waters which resulted in reprisal air attacks against their facilities. Within a few days President Johnson received congressional approval in the form of the *Tonkin Gulf Resolution* to use whatever forces he deemed necessary to counter the growing aggression of North Vietnam.

Shortly after Diem's overthrow and murder, President Kennedy was assassinated in Dallas.

The first US troops in Vietnam were advisors and helicopter pilots. These two advisors are members of the 5th Special Forces Group, the elite "Green Berets". They are wearing the early style non-tropical fatigue uniform. (US Army)

U.S. Ground Troops Arrive

Until 1965 no U.S. ground troops had been sent to Vietnam, although some security and support units had been deployed to guard American installations or provide logistical support to the advisors and helicopter units. By late 1964 the Viet Cong had formed its battalions into regiments and these regiments into divisions. With this structural change many observers felt the VC were shifting to the final "mobile" phase of their guerrilla campaign with the introduction of conventional type organization and tactics against ARVN.

In early 1965 the appearance of regular NVA units gave credence to this theory. As spring approached the tempo of fighting increased dramatically. In addition to attacking ARVN units and positions, the communists began a systematic campaign of terror against US personnel throughout Vietnam. In response to this, the air war against North Vietnam increased dramatically until bombing attacks became an almost daily occurence. In a further response to these attacks against American personnel and installations the decision was made to commit ground troops to provide additional protection. In March the first battalion of a marine regiment landed at Da Nang to guard the sprawling airbase there. Soon the full regiment with its armor and artillery were dug in around the base. Although this commitment of ground troops and the stepped up bombing campaign raised ARVN morale, the VC and the NVA increased their attacks against government positions. By late spring the South Vietnamese were losing the equivalent of a battalion of infantry and a district capital a week to the elusive enemy. Both US leaders and the South Vietnamese government realized that they faced a monumental crisis. Unless massive numbers of American and allied ground troops were immediately committed it was only a matter of time until the communists took control of South Vietnam. In May the United States began to build up its forces to counter the enemy's growing strength and boldness.

The first army unit deployed as a result of this decision was the 173rd Airborne Brigade, the "Sky Soldiers", which were in reserve on Okinawa. They were airlifted into the airfield at Bien Hoa which was located just northeast of Saigon on Route 1. This base was also right next to the notorious War Zone D which the VC used as a staging, supply, and rest area for their attacks against Saigon and the surrounding government positions. With such a major enemy base so close it was inevitable that the VC would react to this new threat to their long held grip on the region. As the "Sky Soldiers" spread out around the base and began patrolling, inquisitive bands of VC observed them and on occasion exchanged small arms fire, resulting in casualties on both sides, the first suffered by army ground troops in Vietnam.

Into War Zone D

General William Westmoreland, the commander of U.S. forces in Vietnam, received authorization to commit his troops against the VC if he felt the situation warranted such action. In response to VC probes around Bien Hoa, he ordered the 173rd to participate in a joint operation with ARVN and Australian troops in an assault on War Zone D, the first such action by US Army troops. Starting on June 28th, 3000 U.S. troops teamed up with Vietnamese airborne units and 800 Australians for a thrust into the communist stronghold. After three futile days the attack was called off because of a lack of substantial contact with the VC. One American was killed and nine were wounded in the operation, but enemy casualties were unknown. And although U.S. soldiers were frustrated at the lack of enemy contact, action would soon increase as more units arrived in-country and began going on the offensive against the communists.

Troop Strength Increases

With the decision to commit U.S. ground forces, additional troops soon followed the "Sky Soldiers" to Vietnam. Shortly after the 173rd's aborted sweep was completed, the 2nd Brigade of the 1st Infantry Division (The Big Red One) began landing at Bien Hoa, as an advance element of the division which would arrive later in the year. This was the first

Members of the 173rd Airborne Brigade move along a road toward defensive positions near Bien Hoa airbase. The two vehicles are mechanical "Mules", a lightweight carrier designed for employment with airborne troops. (US Army)

Defensive positions of the 173rd Airborne Brigade at Bien Hoa during June of 1965. This unit was the first army ground force to be deployed to Vietnam and was initially sent to protect the airbase at Bien Hoa. (US Army)

Two members of the 1st Cav await transportation to their new base near Pleiku in the Central Highlands. Both are wearing the non-tropical uniforms which many of the troops were issued stateside prior to shipping out. These were eventually replaced by lightweight jungle uniforms which were better suited to Vietnam's tropical climate. (US Army)

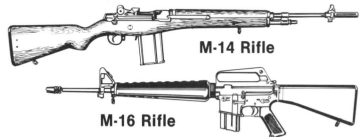

M-14 Rifle

M-16 Rifle

(Above Left) Soldiers of the 1st Infantry Division check for booby traps during a sweep near Bien Hoa. The man on the left carries an old M-3 Grease Gun from World War II. A wide variety of weapons were used early in the war. (US Army)

(Left) A platoon leader from the 1st Infantry Division calls in support against sniper fire near Bien Hoa. The troops are equipped with M-14 rifles which had replaced the M-1 of WWII and had been used extensively in Korea. The M-14 was the standard infantry weapon at the time of the initial troop buildup in Vietnam. (US Army)

deployment of a conventional infantry unit to Vietnam. Close on the heels of the brigade came reinforcements for the 1st Logistical Command which provided support for the various American units already in-country and those scheduled for commitment. Eventually this organization would number close to 50,000 men and although not actually combat troops they often came into contact with the enemy in the various support roles they played.

As these increases raised U.S. troop levels, the VC and NVA continued to escalate the war, bringing in more men and carrying out more attacks. In battles around Quang Nagai city and the area northeast of Saigon ARVN troops suffered over twelve hundred casualties while the enemy's losses were minimal. In Saigon terrorist attacks took a heavy toll of civilian lives and undermined the people's faith in the South Vietnamese government. US and ARVN intelligence identified three NVA regiments, the 18th, 95th, and 101st, as being completely inside South Vietnam. As if to highlight this switch toward conventional tactics the communists launched a multi-battalion attack against the town of Duc Hoa, and chose to stand and slug it out with ARVN troops. This attack showed that the enemy was indeed planning to carry out the final conventional phase of the war before increased US strength could be effectively deployed to shore up the faltering South Vietnamese regime.

To counter this communist strategy more American forces were rushed in-country. At the end of July the 1st Brigade of the 101st Airborne Division, the famous "Screaming Eagles", arrived at Cam Ranh Bay in II Corps. Shortly thereafter, in September, the 1st Cavalry Division (Airmobile) began arriving with its component of helicopters. This division was unique as it was the first airmobile division within the U.S. Army. Unlike other conventional units which relied on mechanized transportation for movement, the 1st Cav used helicopters almost exclusively to move men, artillery, and supplies into battle. The decision to send this unit to Vietnam was based in part on the need to test the airmobile concept under actual battle conditions. If the concept proved valid it would be an invaluable tactic to counter the communists foot mobility in a countryside devoid of adequate road facilities for conventionally equipped forces. Upon its arrival, General Westmoreland decided to move the division into the highlands area to counter the growing communist strength, and intelligence reports of a possible enemy offensive. The division moved from the coast by helicopter to An Khe, a town midway between Pleiku and Qui Nhon along Route 19, and began hacking out a division size base near the small town. To cover the unit's move the 173rd Airborne carried out OPERATION GIBRALTER to protect the cavalrymen and snare any inquisitive VC or NVA. This operation proved more successful than the earlier one in June and in three days of fighting the airborne troops killed over two hundred Viet Cong while taking minimal casualties themselves. Following GIBRALTER, the "Sky Soldiers" withdrew and the 1st Cav. put the finishing touches on their new home. As soon as the base was completed the unit's commander, General Harry Kinnard, began making probes with his helicopters to locate the elusive enemy, but few were found. However, within a short time the NVA would come out of hiding looking for a fight and the airmobile concept would undergo its first real test of battle in a river valley near the Cambodian-Vietnamese border. Here, also, would be tested the merits of a new generation of American infantrymen against a determined and ruthless enemy.

A captain from the 173rd Airborne uses the AN/PRC-25 radio, carried by his radioman, to contact one of his flanking platoons. Both men wear an early version of the jungle fatigue with exposed buttons. (US Army)

First Contact
The Ia Drang Valley

The first significant ground engagement with communist forces occurred during the fall of 1965 in the Ia Drang Valley, southwest of Pleiku, a major city in the Central Highlands. The action began when three NVA regiments, the 32nd, 33rd, and 66th, moved into the area and began preparations for an attack against the Plei Me Special Forces camp in mid-October. While one regiment, the 33rd, surrounded the camp the remaining two laid an ambush for the relief column which they anticipated would be sent from Pleiku once the assault began. The NVA hoped to draw the only ARVN reserves in the highlands area into the trap and completely annihilate the force. After this was accomplished the NVA anticipated an easy victory over the depleted forces at Pleiku and with this the complete control of the Central Highlands. Once this victory was consolidated the NVA command planned to push down to the coast and cut the country in half.

Although the exact nature of the enemy plans were not known at the time, General Westmoreland realized that something was afoot, and moved in elements of the newly arrived 1st Calvary Division. Task Force Ingram, composed of one infantry battalion and one artillery battery, was airlifted into Pleiku to provide assistance in defending the city or relieving the camp. While this move was underway, the division commander obtained permission to move the unit's 1st Brigade to Pleiku where it was to take over Task Force Ingram and carry out its assignment. While this move was afoot, the ARVN relief column attempting to relieve Plei Me was ambushed at two points by the concealed NVA regiments. In reaction to this attack massive air strikes and artillery support from the 1st Cav were called in, with deadly accuracy. Both attacks were repulsed and after hard fighting the column broke through to the camp. To further aid the camp's defenders a number of 1st Cav infantry and artillery units were airlifted into positions around the camp to encircle the NVA forces. Realizing the futility of further contact, the enemy commander disengaged and began pulling his troops back toward the Cambodian border.

In an effort to find the enemy forces the 1st Brigade was ordered to search the area and force the NVA to fight. Although occasional clashes occurred in the last part of October and early November no significant ground contact developed. However, from these contacts and intelligence reports, it was evident that NVA regiments were assembling in the Ia Drang Valley in preparation for another attack on Plei Me. On November 9th the 1st Brigade was replaced by the 3rd Brigade which was ordered to continue the operation. Five days later, on November 14th, the 1st Battalion, 7th Calvary (George Custer's old unit) was airlifted into Landing Zone X-Ray at the southern end of the valley. Although the LZ was not "hot", within an hour contact was made and a prisoner was captured who indicated that the NVA battalions were in the mountains above the LZ. Shortly thereafter the battalion began receiving heavy mortor fire and one platoon became cut off from its parent company. By late afternoon the enemy had surrounded the battalion and made a number of attacks on the three companies holding the LZ. Reinforcements were requested but accurate and intense ground fire drove off the helicopters before another company could be fully unloaded. Throughout the remainder of the day and into the evening

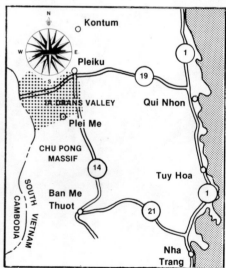

A platoon from the 101st Airborne prepares to board helicopters to aid units of the 1st Infantry Division under attack by the Viet Cong. All are carrying M-26-A1 hand grenades which replaced the old pineapple grenade from World War II. (US Army)

there was a constant seesaw battle as the NVA closed to point-blank range to engage the 1st Cav troopers. Hand to hand fighting took place and after some desperate moments the enemy was finally thrown back. Under cover of darkness reinforcements and supplies were ferried in and wounded were flown out.

A typical Viet Cong booby trap. Sharpened bamboo spikes, called punji stakes, were emplaced at the bottom of a hole and then covered over with vegetation in the hope that some soldier would step on them. Often the VC coated these with human or animal waste to make them septic. (US Army)

Throughout the remainder of the night and into the next day the fighting raged. With the aid of artillery and air support these attacks were beaten back and finally, in the early afternoon, the battalion was able to push out of the perimeter. Enemy bodies were found stacked like cordwood behind great ant hills and a large quantity of weapons and equipment was captured. The unit which had been cut off was recovered, and, as evening approached the battalion consolidated its position with another battalion that had reinforced it. A quiet night passed but in the morning when the men had their "mad minute fire"*, it prematurely triggered an enemy attack which was easily beaten off. With this last flurry of enemy activity the initial battle of the Ia Drang Valley was over. In the three days of heavy fighting the 1st Battalion had killed 634 NVA soldiers, taken six prisoners, and captured large stores of weapons, supplies, and equipment. The cost had been high, however. The battalion had lost seventy-nine troopers killed and 121 wounded. But despite these losses the "green" troopers of the 1st Cav had stood up to veteran NVA units and had come out on top.

Through the remainder of November the 3rd Brigade, and, later the 2nd Brigade, prowled amongst the peaks and valleys of the Ia Drang. Constant fighting raged as the calvary troopers found the elusive enemy. By the last week of November the NVA had enough. The remaining NVA troops retreated across the border into Cambodia. OPERATION SILVER BAYONET, as this action was code-named, eventually resulted in almost 1,800 enemy dead, against 240 U.S. fatalities, but while these numbers were impressive a large part of the enemy force was able to find sanctuary in Cambodia from where it posed a constant threat to the Central Highlands.

1966: The Tempo Increases

Following the stunning defeat of the communists in the Ia Drang Valley, US forces began to increase their offensive operations against the enemy in an effort to seize the initiative. By the beginning of 1966 the 3rd Brigade of the 25th Infantry Division had arrived in-country and set up its base at Pleiku. In January the brigade teamed up with the 173rd Airborne and an Australian battalion to sweep areas near the Cambodian border. Only limited contact was made although large quantities of weapons and ammunition were seized. In the months which followed the VC and NVA proved reluctant to engage U.S. troops. Perhaps the lessons of the Ia Drang were still being digested, but in the first half of 1966 there were few large scale attacks on American forces. Most of the search and destroy operations encountered little enemy oppositions as the communists evaded contact. The most significant operation of this period was OPERATION MASHER/WHITE WINGS/THANG PHONG II carried out by the 1st Cavalry Division along with Marine, ARVN and Republic of Korea (ROK) units from the end of January to the beginning of March. This action was the first large scale operation across corps boundries and resulted in over 2300 known enemy casualties.

As summer approached the action began to increase. In the Central Highlands the 25th Infantry and 101st Airborne carried out OPERATION PAUL REVERE and HAWTHORNE which resulted in over 1000 North Vietnamese dead. North of Saigon the 1st Infantry Division swept Binh Long province in search of the 9th VC Division during OPERATION El PASO II. This sweep lasted one and a half months and killed at least 850 Viet Cong. The summer also saw a major increase in U.S. ground troops with the arrival in August of advance elements of the 4th Infantry Division. These reinforcements raised the total U.S. troop level to over 350,000 men.

While this increase was occurring, the 196th Infantry Brigade began OPERATION ATTLEBORO, a search and destroy mission in War Zone C during mid-September. At first no significant contacts developed, but in October a major base camp was uncovered in the area. At the same time intelligence reports indicated that the 9th VC Division, which had been mauled by the 1st Infantry Division during El PASO II, had moved into the area from its sanctuaries in Cambodia. To aid the 196th in their search, elements of the 1st Infantry Division moved into War Zone C. On October 28th they made contact with a VC battalion and uncovered a number of base camps. By the first week of November it was apparent

*All troops sprayed the surrounding trees and brush for a minute with small arm fire to kill any enemy infiltrators or snipers who had infiltrated during the night.

9

A platoon leader awaits orders to move out during a sweep near Bong Son. The early uniforms these men wear were hot and uncomfortable compared to the jungle fatigues which were designed to replace them. (US Army)

M-59 Baseball Grenade

M26A1 Fragmentation Grenade

M18 SMOKE VIOLET

M-185 Smoke Grenade

M-34 White Phosphorous Grenade

M-127 Signal Flare

SIGNAL ILLUMINATION, GROUND PARACHUTE, M127, WHITE STAR (HAND HELD)

(Above Left) A howitzer crew prepares to fire in support of the 1st Cavalry Division during OPERATION MASHER. They have yet to receive the lightweight jungle fatigues which were characterized by large pockets on both the shirt and pants. (US Army)

A trooper from the 101st Airborne lays down covering fire against enemy soldiers hidden in the treeline. He is carrying extra belts of machine gun ammunition and an M-72 Lightweight Anti-tank Weapon (LAW), a throwaway rocket launcher. (US Army)

A company from the 1st Infantry Division (The Big Red One) move down a road near Tay Ninh prior to a sweep in War Zone C. The closest soldier carries an M-60 machine gun and extra rounds of ammunition. (US Army)

(Above Left) An engineer from the 25th Infantry Division prepares explosives to destroy a communist bunker. Bunkers like these were hard to spot unless troops were very close to them. An M-79 grenade launcher is to the left of the engineer. (US Army)

that a very substantial enemy force was in the area. To back up units already in the field, brigades from the 4th and 25th Infantry Divisions, and the 173rd Airborne Brigade were brought in. This made ATTLEBORO the largest U.S. ground operation to date. Throughout November the fighting raged as the various units tried to encircle the elusive Viet Cong. By the end of November the communists had lost 2200 dead and 900 wounded in ground fighting and air strikes. What was left of the 9th Division slipped back over the border to Cambodia. Friendly losses amounted to 150 killed and 500 wounded.

As ATTLEBORO neared completion, OPERATION IRVING was initiated north of the coastal city of Qui Nhon. The purpose of this drive was to clear the populated coastal region of the Viet Cong's political and military structure. On D-Day, October 2nd, two brigades of the 1st Cavalry made helicopter assaults inside a pocket ringed by ARVN and Korean forces. Fierce fighting erupted around the village of Hoa Hoi and raged on for two days. When the village was finally captured, 233 of the enemy were dead or wounded, while American losses were 3 killed and 29 wounded. As the operation progressed the cavalry troopers constantly shifted positions by means of their helicopters. This kept the guerrillas off-balance and constantly on the move. By the time the sweep was terminated on October 24th over 680 VC or NVA had died and more then 740 had been captured. Total losses for the 1st Cav amounted to 20 killed in action. IRVING effectively eliminated the influence of the VC in this area, which had a lasting effect on the Pacification Program.

As 1966 drew to a close the newly arrived 4th Infantry Division, along with support from the 25th Infantry and 1st Cavalry Divisions, conducted PAUL REVERE IV, west of Pleiku. In sweeps along the Cambodian border contact with communist forces was almost a daily occurrence. Unfortunately, with their border sanctuaries so close, the enemy would make sudden attacks and then pull back into Cambodia since U.S. troops could not continue contact once they reached the border. Nevertheless in the six week operation which ended on December 30th the NVA lost over 1000 men while American losses were minimal. As the year closed, the 9th Infantry Division began arriving during mid-December and was deployed in III Corps, raising US troop strength to 385,000.

An engineer uses a mine detector to search for weapons and booby traps in a pile of rice stalks. The Viet Cong were masters at concealment and the placement of booby traps. (US Army)

Troops from the 25th Infantry stand security as members of their squad search for Viet Cong during OPERATION MAKAHA. Closest soldier has on jungle fatigues and wears a towel around his neck to soak up sweat. (US Army)

(Above Left) Members of the 101st Airborne, aboard a C-130 transport, relax as they fly to a new base during the spring of 1966. The soldier on the "Mule" wears a tiger striped camouflage uniform, a rather uncommon outfit for regular combat troops. (USAF)

Rucksack Frames

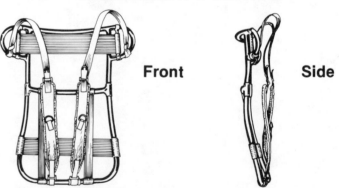

Front   **Side**

A good portion of a soldiers time is spent waiting. These men from the 173rd Airborne rest while they wait for helicopters to take them on an air assault. The tubular items are rucksack frames for ease in carrying equipment. (US Army)

A radioman looks for signs of the Cong in an abandoned farm house in Phuoc Long province. The patch on the shoulder is that of the 25th Infantry Division, a Yellow lightning bolt on a Red crest. Such colorful insignias were soon discarded because they could betray a man's position in the Green foliage. They were replaced with low visibility patches that used only the colors Black and Green. (US Army)

A little humor at Nha Trang. As in past wars, American soldiers had a sense of humor and the Vietnam war was no different. (US Army)

Flak Jacket

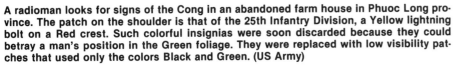

Front   Back

A column of grunts from the 25th Infantry move along a road near the village of Cu Chi during OPERATION FORT SMITH. First man on the left wears a flak jacket designed to stop shrapnel and small arms fire, though leaving it unzipped opens up a large area of vital organs. He carries a M-18 smoke grenade on his belt. Man on the right is armed with an M-79 grenade launcher. (US Army)

13

Members of an infantry unit usually had to carry extra ammunition or mortar rounds when on operations. This soldier from the 173rd Airborne carries five mortar rounds in addition to his own field gear. In the hot, tropical climate of Vietnam this kind of load could very quickly sap the strength of the strongest man. (US Army)

(Above Right) A squad from the 27th Infantry, the "Wolfhounds", move through a rice paddy near Cu Chi. A wide variety of weapons are carried by this squad. The closest man has an M-16, the next an M-14, the next two M-79 grenade launchers, and the remainder carry M-14s. This unit was attached to the 25th Infantry Division. (US Army)

A Long Range Reconnaissance Patrol (LRRP, pronounced lirp) from the 25th Infantry move in the shadows while on a patrol out of Cu Chi. Besides wearing the tiger striped camouflaged fatigues notice how the first two men's M-16s are also painted in camouflage colors. These uniforms proved very efficient in the dense jungles of Vietnam where light was let in through the numerous layers of leaves. (US Army)

The dense jungle conditions which US troops faced in Vietnam can be seen as troopers of the 1st Cav carry out OPERATION THAYER II near Qui Nhon. (US Army)

(Above Left) A soldier searches a haystack for possible hidden weapons or supplies. Often times the VC would booby trap such things with explosives or poisonous snakes to discourage such searches. The soldier is armed with a shotgun which was seldom seen in the field. He also carries both fragmentary and smoke grenades. (US Army)

A machinegun team fires on a suspected enemy position during a sweep by the 196th Light Infantry Brigade near Tay Ninh. The gunner is holding the M-60 with a special glove to protect his hand from the hot barrel. A sling was usually attached to the gun which ran over the shoulder to help in balancing the weapon.

Engineers of the 1st Infantry Division clear a road south of Quan Loi. The men wear flak jackets in case a mine is remotely triggered by the enemy. The third man back carries cord to explode any mines which are uncovered. The men are carrying a mixture of weapons including a shotgun. (US Army)

(Above Right) Even with constant sweeps the enemy proved adept at setting up mines. The jeep in the background detonated an anti-tank mine. The force of the explosion threw bodies nearly three hundred feet. (US Army)

M-60 Machine Gun
7.62 мм

While a comrade keeps watch two soldiers fill their canteens from a jungle stream. Thirst was a constant companion to troops as they prowled through the hot, steaming jungle. Note the extra belts of machinegun ammunition carried by the two men in the stream and the towel around the neck of the man keeping guard. (US Army)

16

In Vietnam the unexpected usually happened. In this instance a soldier from the 101st Airborne hastily moves his gear out of the way of an approaching herd of cattle. The lightweight rucksack frame saw widespread usage in Vietnam. (US Army)

(Above Left) A patrol from the 25th Infantry crosses a crude log bridge constructed by the North Vietnamese near the Cambodian border. Along with troops of the newly arrived 4th Infantry Division, they are taking part in "OPERATION PAUL REVERE IV". (US Army)

M-60 Machine Gun on Tripod

Because of the nature of guerrilla warfare, military police were often used to keep roads open or patrol roads between bases. These MPs from the 1st Cav move along a road northeast of An Khe. (US Army)

Elements of the 101st Airborne unload at Kontum in the Central Highlands. The guitar does not appear to be government issued equipment. Note the mixture of jungle fatigues and older utility uniforms among these troops. (US Army)

(Above Right) Paratroopers from the 173rd Airborne Brigade hitch a ride on an M-113. Note how all the men carry extra ammo belts for the squad's machine gun. (US Army)

Helmets

Tanker **Standard Helmet** **Helmet with Camouflage Cover**

Viet Cong suspects are interrogated by members of the 503rd Regiment, 173rd Airborne Brigade, near the village of Vo Dat. M-113 in background has one of the early armored shields for the commander. (US Army)

Into The Iron Triangle

With the NVA stopped in their tracks by the influx of US combat troops, General Westmoreland began to launch counterattacks against the reeling enemy forces. In early 1967, he decided to launch an assault against the area north of Saigon between War Zone C ad D. Known as the "Iron Triangle", it was a jungle redoubt of dense forests, tangled underbrush, and hundreds of miles of tunnels and bunkers. The area had first served as a haven for the Viet Minh during the Japanese occupation and again during the French recolonization attempt. It had been further developed as the Viet Cong began their war against the Diem regime. In over twenty years a massive labyrinth of shelters, tunnels, hospitals, armories, command posts and fighting positions had evolved through the work of thousand of soldiers and laborers. Over the years the Iron Triangle had acquired a fearsome reputation and prior to the arrival of US troops, ARVN forces only entered the area in massive numbers.

The first attempt to destroy the redoubt by U.S. troops occurred in late 1965 when the 173rd Airborne Brigade, along with Australian and New Zealand troops, tried to crack it as part of their incursion into War Zone D. Unfortunately, little contact was made, and damage to the jungle fortress was minimal. After this failure, the VC and NVA rebuilt the few areas that the 173rd had destroyed and continued to mount attacks from the region, while at the same time using it as a rest and resupply point for field units.

To eliminate this dreaded citadel once and for all, Westmoreland launched OPERATION CEDAR FALLS, on 8 January 1967, with a surprise assault on the village of Ben Suc. This village, of approximately 6,000 people, was a fortified enemy supply and political center which the VC had controlled since 1964. In order to achieve surprise, a battalion of the 1st Infantry Division made a dawn helicopter landing in the middle of the village without supporting fire. The unit, commanded by Colonel Alexander Haig*, moved swiftly to secure the area around the town and kill or capture any VC who attempted to break out. While this was going on, the 25th Infantry Division and 196th Infantry Brigade moved into blocking positions along the western edge of the triangle, while to the east and north the 1st Infantry Division, the 173rd Airborne Brigade, and 11th Armored Cavalry Regiment blocked escape routes in those directions. Once these units had encircled the "Iron Triangle" they set about to destroy it. On the second day of the battle the 11th Armored Cav thrust into the region from the east while a battalion of the 1st Infantry and 173rd Airborne made an airmobile assault in the north. In a few short days the various units involved had crisscrossed the region and cut it into a number of isolated sections. But action was light as the equivalent of two enemy regiments had either scattered or fled the area without making a stand. Although the operation ran for three weeks, enemy losses amounted to a little over 700, while US losses numbered 72. The total number of troops committed was considerable, but the results were rather disappointing.

However, OPERATION CEDAR FALLS was not intended to kill enemy troops but rather to render the Iron Triangle unusable. Once the area had been secured, engineers moved into the region and began to alter the face of the fortress. The vast underground tunnel complex and chambers were searched by "tunnel rats". These were small statured G.I.s who volunteered to explore the vast network of passageways despite the dangers of booby traps, poison snakes, and an enemy who knew every turn and room in this subterranean world. These volunteers slowly cleared what they could with explosives which rendered many parts of the complex useless to the communists. Topside, the engineers cut and burned the tangled undergrowth and demolished any structures or bunkers they found. The entire population of the region was relocated so they could no longer aid the NVA or VC. By the end of January the job was done. The Iron Triangle lay covered in a pall of smoke, its surface bare of vegetation, and pitted with collapsed tunnels and destroyed bunkers. It seemed that the fortress would never again plague Allied forces. But even as the last troops withdrew, figures arose antlike from untouched tunnel complexes and began the job of rebuilding the redoubt. Like a mythical Phoenix, the Iron Triangle would rise from its ashes to plague the allied forces at a later date.

*Colonel Alexander Haig became General Alexander Haig and eventually Secretary of State Alexander Haig.

Junction City — A Turning Point

Hard on the heels of CEDAR FALLS came OPERATION JUNCTION CITY, one of the largest ground actions US forces undertook during the entire war. Involved in this massive operation were units of the 1st, 4th, 9th, and 25th Infantry Divisions, the 11th Armored Cavalry Regiment, and the 196th Infantry and 173rd Airborne Brigades, along with ARVN and Australian troops. Over 45,000 men took part in this ground action which focused on War Zone C, a triangular shaped portion of jungle northwest of Saigon which abutted the Cambodian border. Intelligence officers believed that the 9th VC Division, 10,000 men strong, and several NVA battalions, plus numerous base camps, hospitals, supply depots, and weapons factories were located within this zone. Although this operation had been scheduled earlier, CEDAR FALLS had taken precedence over it when new intelligence information had been discovered about enemy units in the Iron Triangle. Upon the completion of CEDAR FALLS plans were finalized for encircling War Zone C and crushing any communist units in the area under the code name OPERATION JUNCTION CITY.

The portion of War Zone C which JUNCTION CITY took place was west of An Loc, north of Tay Ninh, and extended to roughly the Cambodian border. The overall plan called for allied units to form a horseshoe-shaped position around this area, blocking avenues of retreat while other forces drove up from the horseshoe's open southern end. Intially the operation was to have two phases but as the action progressed a third was added to take advantage of tactical conditions. In the first phase the 1st Infantry Division, augmented by troops from the 173rd Airborne Brigade, the 1st Cavalry Regiment, Task Force Wallace (ARVN), and the 9th Infantry Division, had the responsibility for the eastern and northern portions of the horseshoe. The responsibility for the northwestern and western sections of the perimeter was assigned to the 25th Infantry Division. To aid the division in this task, units from the 4th Infantry Division, the 196th Light Infantry Brigade, the 11th Armored Cavalry Regiment, and Task Force Alpha (Vietnamese Marines) were allocated to its commander. In the south the open end of the horseshoe would be sealed by a brigade from the 25th Infantry and elements of the 11th Armored Cavalry. These units also had the job of

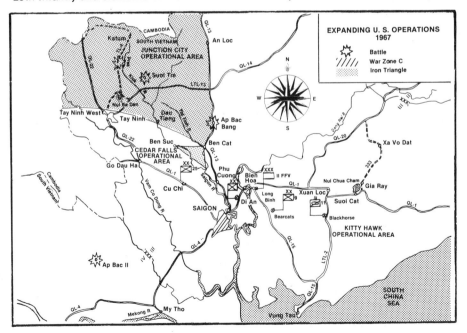

19

driving northward into the horseshoe and forcing the enemy against the blocking forces, a tactic labeled the "hammer and anvil".

The operation began on 22 February when elements of the 1st Infantry made a series of airmobile assaults near the Cambodian border. Shortly afterwards a battalion of the 173rd Airborne made the only parachute assault of the war when it jumped near the village of Katum on the eastern side of the horseshoe. Within a short time the battalion had achieved its objectives with few casualties and began receiving heavy equipment drops. The other units involved in the operation then commenced moving into positions around the horseshoe, while the "hammer" units from the south began their northward drive. By day's end all units were in place or moving into place. But little enemy resistance was encountered. Only twice during this phase, on 28 February and 10 March near Prek Klok, would there be any substantial contact with the communists. During the first battle a battalion of the 9th VC division attacked a company from the 1st Infantry which was sweeping the jungle south of Prek Klok. In the ensuing fight portions of the company were cut off. To relieve them both, air and artillery support, along with additional reinforcements, were called in. By the end of the day the company had been extracted but it suffered over fifty dead or wounded. The enemy losses totalled nearly two hundred, many of them killed by air and artillery strikes. Two weeks later two other battalions from the 9th VC staged an attack on an artillery fire base located at Prek Klok. At the base were two artillery batteries, a mechanized infantry battalion*, and some engineers. Shortly after sundown on 10 March, the VC began to bombard the position with mortars, rockets and recoilless rifle fire. Despite heavy US return fire from mortars, artillery, and from the M-113s, the enemy launched a major assault against the eastern perimeter and diversionary probes at other points. For over an hour hard fighting ensued, with the defenders calling in air, artillery, and gunship support. The communists were able to destroy a number of M-113s but did not breach the perimeter. Sporadic fire continued through the night but after the initial attack the VC withdrew. Over 200 VC were killed in this battle while the US losses were 3 killed and 38 wounded. This battle marked the last significant contact of phase one which ended a week after, on 17 March.

During the second phase of JUNCTION CITY the horseshoe was gradually tightened. As the area the enemy had to maneuver in decreased, contact increased. As a result, the fighting during this phase was far more intense, particularly in the first few days of the new attack. On March 19th, a battalion from the 4th Infantry Division suffered numerous casualties near Suoi Tre when the VC detonated five remote controlled land mines during an airmobile assault. These destroyed or damaged 9 helicopters and killed or wounded 48 soldiers. The next day, troops from the 273rd VC Regiment made a human wave attack against a fire support base near Ap Bau Bang which contained one artillery battery and a armored cavalry troop. The VC were able to penetrate the perimeter at several places after an intense bombardment. In some cases the enemy swarmed over tanks and APCs, and hand-to-hand fighting took place. Eventually, with air strikes, artillery support, fire from gunships, and relief forces the enemy was forced back with over 200 killed while US dead were 3.

The next night, at Fire Base Gold, near Suoi Tre, the 272nd VC Regiment made a desperate assault against the one infantry and two artillery battalions stationed there. In the early morning hours the communists began smothering the base with mortar, rocket, and recoilless rifle fire. Over 1000 rounds impacted on the camp before the VC began their assault. In hard fighting they broke through the eastern perimeter at a number of points and forced the soldiers back. Despite support fire the Americans were unable to drive the enemy back, even when they fired their own artillery at point blank range. The fighting intensified until the VC were within hand grenade range of the command post. Fortunately, a mechanized and armored battalion were able to break through at this critical moment. As the tanks and APCs broke through the encircling VC troops, the enemy swarmed over the vehicles but were thrown off in hand-to-hand combat. With these welcome reinforcements the base defenders rallied and eventually threw the VC back. Losses were staggering. Over 600 enemy dead lay on the field while US losses were 31 killed and 109 wounded. It was an outstanding victory achieved by the sheer courage and tenacity of the American soldier who fought there.

The last major battle of the second phase took place at Ap Gu near the Cambodian border. Two battalions from the 1st Infantry Division staged an airmobile assault into the area on 30 March, initially encountering no opposition. The next day a platoon on patrol was ambushed, and, as a relief company went to its aid, the VC sprang an ambush with a full battalion from the 271st VC Regiment. Eventually, another company was needed to rescue the two pinned down units. As the units withdrew into night defensive positions the two battalion commanders prepared for a possible night attack. Their instincts proved correct. In the early morning hours of 1 April, three enemy battalions from the 271st VC Regiment attacked the perimeter of the battalion commanded by Lieutenant Colonel Alexander Haig. Other VC units made diversionary attacks on the second battalion and on nearby artillery fire bases. In savage fighting the communists were able to force back one company, but reinforcements moved in and stabilized the situation. By daylight the defenders were able to rally, and with the aid of air and artillery support, drove the VC back into the jungle. Though U.S. units tried to encircle the retreating enemy, the elusive Cong slipped away, but not before leaving behind 500 dead on the battlefield. The two battalions of US Infantry suffered 17 killed and 102 wounded during the hour long battle. However, as further patrols probed the surrounding jungle an additional 100 enemy dead were found. These losses effectively crippled the enemy regiment, and it would be months before it was ready for combat again.

The final phase of JUNCTION CITY began on 16 April, but by this time there were few enemy troops left in the small area not yet searched. Thus, only scattered resistance was encountered by US and allied forces, and no significant contacts resulted. In mid-May the US Command terminated the operation because of lack of contact and the need to shift ground forces to counteract enemy probes in other sectors. The final results of JUNCTION CITY were impressive. Nearly 3,000 troops from the 9th VC Division had been killed while over 200 had been captured or rallied to the allied side. In addition, nearly 100 base camps were destroyed, and large amounts of weapons, ammunition and supplies had been seized. But this had not been achieved without cost. American personnel losses amounted to 282 killed and 1,576 wounded, along with material losses in armor, artillery, and helicopters. War Zone C was not completely destroyed. Though severely damaged it would again be rebuilt from the ashes and continue to be a thorn in the side of the US and ARVN forces. But, the VC had learned that even in such a jungle redoubt as this they were not safe from the ever increasing ground power of US forces.

*Equipped with M-113 Armored Personnel Carriers.

A machinegun team from the 173rd Airborne moves into position during OPERATION CEDAR FALLS. Note how the gunner has positioned his pistol for the protection of a rather delicate area, and the use of a sling to help in carrying the M-60. (US Army)

Company commanders from the 3rd Brigade, 25th Infantry, discuss a tunnel complex which their troops have just uncovered during CEDAR FALLS. Note the baggy pockets of the jungle fatigues and M59 baseball grenade carried by the pointing officer. These did not see widespread usage until later in the war when they began replacing the old "pineapple grenades" which ARVN used extensivley. (US Army)

Soldiers watch as supplies and heavy equipment are dropped during OPERATION JUNCTION CITY. This was the only large scale airborne assault mounted by American forces during the war. (USAF)

Men from the 1st Infantry Division hitch a ride on an M-48 tank from the 4th Cavalry during JUNCTION CITY. This operation took place in War Zone "C" during the early months of 1967. (US Army)

A machinegunner from the 35th Infantry Regiment, 25th Infantry Division, struggles up a steep hillside near Phu Cat. He carries a variety of equipment including an entrenching tool, machete or K bar, extra bandoliers of ammunition, and a climbing rope. (US Army)

Careful movement through tangled vegetation reduced the chances of setting off booby traps. Members of the 9th Infantry Division slowly move through a row of dense bushes near Dong Tam in the Mekong Delta. This unit was the first large US ground force to be sent into the Delta. (US Army)

These soldiers from the 196th Light Infantry Brigade move through a flooded area near their base camp at Chu Lai. The lack of extra gear indicates that this is a very local patrol which will return home before night. (US Army)

A soldier checks the magazine of his M-16 to be sure it has no dirt or rust which might cause it to jam. Though a good weapon, the M-16 needed constant cleaning to prevent jamming. The standard magazine held twenty rounds but most troops only put in eighteen so as not to weaken the magazine spring. If this happened the last round or two would not seat properly. (U.S. Army)

(Above Left) Dog handlers from the 199th Infantry Brigade conduct a search during a sweep north of Saigon. Police dogs were helpful in locating weapons and ammunition, but they were unable to cope with the extremely hot climate, which restricted their usage except for local operations. (US Army)

A squad leader from the 1st Cav prepares to call his company commander during OPERATION MALHEUR in Quang Nai provence. The radio telephone operator (RTO) was a vital link in the communications setup and a prime target for enemy snipers. RTO's suffered a high percentage of casualties during the initial stages of a battle or firefight. (US Army)

An RTO plods through a marsh in the Mekong delta near Rach Kien. These conditions were typical of the area and resulted in most operations being limited to less than a week. This allowed the troops to dry out and cut down on foot and skin infections which could put troops out of action as sure as a bullet wound. (US Army)

(Above Right) Men of the 1st Cav move along a jungle stream during a search and destroy mission in the An Lao valley. Because of the dense jungle, streams were often the easiest way to move. Unfortunately the enemy often laid booby traps or ambushes along them because of this constant use by American troops. (US Army)

A platoon leader calls a halt with hand signals while a detail goes forward to check out a suspicious area. Note the extra smoke grenades on the back of the radio and the compass on the pocket of the platoon leader. (US Army)

An M-79 grenadier from the 2nd Brigade, 1st Infantry Division, loads his M-79 grenade launcher during an engagement with enemy forces during August of 1965 near Bien Hoa. This was one of the first operations against the enemy by U.S. forces in the war.

A sergeant from the 199th Infantry Brigade searches a haystack near the village of Binh Chanh in 1967. He is carrying an M-79 grenade launcher and wears a pith helmet.

A paratrooper from the 173rd Airborne Brigade prior to the only parachute assault of the Vietnam War by a regular army unit. This took place during operation JUNCTION CITY in late February of 1967.

A soldier equipped with an M-72 LAW taking a break during a sweep near An Khe in December of 1965. He is wearing a poncho to keep out the rain.

A sergeant from the 1st Brigade, 101st Airborne Division, prepares to blow an abandoned V.C. bunker during operation VAN BUREN in January of 1966. Camouflage uniforms were not common among most field units during this stage of the war.

Long Range Reconnaissance Patrol (LRRP) from the 173rd Airborne Brigade in the Central Highlands, 1967. He is wearing a "Tiger Stripe" uniform which many soldiers felt was the most effective camouflage design for this type of pattern.

A soldier from the 9th Infantry Division questions a suspected VC in the Mekong Delta during the spring of 1967. Helmet graffiti became very popular as the war progressed.

A soldier from the 8th Infantry, 4th Infantry Division, prepares to move out on a reconnaissance patrol near Dak To. His pants legs are tied to keep the leeches from crawling up his legs.

A machinegun team from the 199th Infantry Brigade takes a break at Fire Support Base Mace during late 1969. As the war dragged on, many soldiers took to wearing flowers on their uniforms or equipment as a sign of protest.

Members of the 9th Infantry Division, attached to the Riverine force ford a stream during a search and destroy mission in the delta. Such watercourses as these crisscrossed the region and made movement extremely difficult. (US Army)

(Above Right) A machinegunner passes his M-60 to an RTO who is on a little more solid ground, in the hope that without the extra weight he can extract himself from the glue-like mud he is bogged down in. Notice how both men use the band on their helmets to hold cigarettes and other items which they wish to keep dry and have easy access. (US Army)

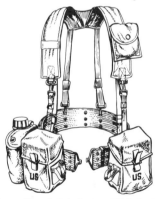

Harness

Canteen

A patrol from the 1st Infantry Division moves into the brush near their base during OPERATION BILLINGS in Phuoc Long province. The use of camouflage hats and scarves is unusual with regular jungle fatigues. The closest man carries a CAR-15, a shortened version of the M-16, with a telescopic stock. (US Army)

On The Offensive

Following JUNCTION CITY, US troops began a series of operations designed to root out hard core VC and NVA units throughout Vietnam. In response to increased enemy activity in I Corps elements of the 25th Infantry, 101st Airborne, and 196th Brigade relocated to the area to help the hard pressed marines. These units came under the control of Task Force Oregon, a provisional division size organization which later became the Americal Division. While this shift occurred, additional US troops arrived in-country to form the Mobile Riverine Force (MRF) in the Mekong Delta, the first large scale deployment of American forces to this area. Because of the vast system of waterways in this region the troops, from the 9th Infantry Division, were based on shallow drafted barracks ships and moved into battle aboard specially modified landing craft. Other landing craft were fitted with heavier armament, helipads, and special communications to provide support in the narrow channels and swamps which characterized the region. In March the MRF began a series of operations to clear the VC from the Rung Sat, a dense mangrove swamp southeast of Saigon. These initial operations proved successful and vindicated the riverine concept. By the middle of the summer the entire complement of troops and ships were ready for full scale operations, and the force set up its headquarters at Don Tam near the district capital of My Tho. From here the unit carried out between six and eight search and destroy mission per month.

Throughout the summer and fall of 1967 US troops were constantly on the move, carrying out numerous sweeps against suspected communist troop concentrations. Many of these were non-productive since the enemy rarely fought unless he had a decided advantage. Instead, the guerrillas relied on ambushes, booby traps, and sniper fire to counter the much stronger US units. However, some operations were able to pin the communists down, and when this occurred the enemy lost heavily. In September Task Force Oregon accounted for nearly 2000 VC or NVA dead during OPERATION WHEELER in I Corps. Further south, OPERATIONS BOLLING and SHENANDOAH II, conducted by the 1st Cavalry Division, the 173rd Airborne Brigade, and the 1st Infantry Division cost the communists 1600 casualties. In the Mekong Delta the MRF carried out CORONADO V which netted over 300 guerrilla dead. Operations such as these pushed the Viet Cong and North Vietnamese away from the major population centers, but as the enemy withdrew toward their border sanctuaries in Cambodia and Laos they received reinforcements and supplies which enabled them to rebuild their shattered formations. Within a relatively short time these same units were operating again.

The Border Battles: Dak To

In the late fall of 1967 three engagements took place along the Vietnamese-Laotion-Cambodian borders which became collectively known as the Border Battles. The first one involved elements of an ARVN battalion near Song Be in Phuoc Long Province, northeast of Saigon. In the last week of October a NVA regiment tried to wrestle the town from the Vietnamese troops but were beaten back with over a hundred dead and scores of wounded. A few days later, on 29 October, another NVA regiment attempted to take the town of Loc Ninh in the province of Binh Long, immediately to the west of Song Be. Unlike Song Be, Loc Ninh was defended by local troops, and the NVA felt the town would fall easily. Much to their surprise these locals not only held out but inflicted serious losses on the NVA troops until being reinforced by two ARVN companies.

To forestall further NVA attacks in this area a brigade of the 1st Infantry Division joined with ARVN troops in a sweep of the countryside. As part of SHENANDOAH II, this operation was designed to clear the enemy out of the rubber plantations around Loc Ninh. In the long rows of evenly spaced rubber trees the NVA soldiers had wide, unobstructed fields of fire which gave them a definite advantage over the assaulting US and ARVN troops. However, with the judicious use of artillery, aircraft, and armor, the tables were

Flamethrowers were not used extensively in Vietnam because of their weight and a scarcity of suitable targets. Here a member of the 1st Cav uses one to clear out a cave in the An Lao valley. Gas mask protects him from the smoke and noxious fumes given off by the weapon. (US Army)

These troops have just disembarked from the landing craft in the background and are moving along the top of a paddy dike. The water level in this area is right at the surface as evidenced by the river in the background. Movement along the tops of dikes like this made it easy for the enemy to slow down the advance with a single machinegun or sniper. (US Army)

turned on the enemy and almost a thousand NVA soldiers perished in the vicious fighting. Unfortunately, not all the fighting was so one sided. Just south of Loc Ninh near where the Iron Triangle and War Zone C merge, a battalion from the 1st Infantry ran into one of the most devastating ambushes American forces encountered in the war. While on patrol the battalion walked into a carefully laid trap set up by an entire NVA regiment. Without warning the battalion was hit from all sides by intense small arms and mortar fire. In this initial attack, a large number of officers were killed, including the battalion commander and a number of his staff. The unit was able to dig in and resist further attacks until help arrived. Over a hundred US soldiers were killed or wounded. The NVA regiment managed to slip away with minimal losses before reinforcements could move to block its escape.

However these initial battles were but a prelude to the bloodiest fighting since the Ia Drang valley campaign. Dak To was a small Green Beret outpost nestled in a river valley near the junction of the Cambodian-Laotion border with Vietnam. It sat along Highway 14, the main north-south road in the Central Highlands. In addition it was also astride Route 512 which served as a major Viet Cong and NVA infiltration line into the highlands area. In late October fragmentary intelligence reports indicated that the NVA high command was moving the reinforced 1st NVA division toward the town. To forestall any attempt by the enemy in this direction the 4th Infantry Division mounted operation MACARTHUR in the vicinity of Dak To. Almost immediately an NVA sergeant defected to US forces with detailed plans of the enemies intentions. Though at first skeptical US officers were finally able to confirm the soldiers story which proved surprisingly accurate. The NVA plan called for two regiments, the 32nd and 66th, to attack Dak To from the south and southeast, while another, the 24th, would assault the town from the northeast. The remaining regiment, the 174th would remain in reserve. To counter this plan, the 4th Infantry moved a number of battalions, including one from the 173rd Airborne Brigade into blocking positions around Dak To along the main NVA attack route. Once these units were in position they began to probe the surrounding hills in search of the enemy. Almost immediately the battalion in the south ran into heavy enemy resistance. To counter this, massive air strikes, including B-52s, and artillery fire were called in on the NVA position. More battalions were airlifted in to join the vicious battle. The bloody fighting see-sawed back and forth until mid-November when the NVA commander finally realized his forces were no match for the American troops with their supporting fire. In an attempt to extricate his shattered regiments the enemy committed the reserve regiment to cover a retreat to the southwest where US forces had been helicoptered into blocking positions.

The 174th NVA regiment chose to make a stand on Hill 875, so named for its height above sea level. In a short time the enemy had dug a series of deep interconnecting bunkers on the steep, wooded slopes. These positions were discovered by a patrol from a battalion of the 173rd Airborne Brigade. While supporting fire hit the bunker complex the battalion began advancing up the rugged slope. Despite support fire the battalion was hit with such intense and accurate defensive fire that it was pinned down, and suffered very heavy casualties. In an attempt to relieve the battalion another unit was brought in by helicopter but fierce ground fire drove them off. Eventually, a combination of air and artillery support suppressed the ground fire so that the battalion could relieve its sister unit. For four days these two battalions from the 173rd, later joined by another battalion from the 4th Infantry Division, fought a desperate battle with the 174th for control of the rocky outcrop. At times the combat was so close that no support fire could be delivered. Finally, the NVA could no longer hold out and the weary US troops took the hilltop on Thanksgiving Day. The capture of Hill 875 marked the end of the "Border Battles". In the fighting around Dak To the four NVA regiments lost over 1600 men killed plus a large number who were seriously wounded. Nearly 300 American soldiers also perished in the bitter fighting, but the enemy drive to capture this vital area was thwarted.

As this battle in the Central Highlands ended, more reinforcements continued to flow into Vietnam. The major ground units contained in this deployment was the 101st Airborne Division, the famous "Screaming Eagles". Their arrival increased overall US troop strength to over 485,000 men. This number raised the total American strength to a level greater than that used in the Korean War. Events in 1968 would soon show that even more men would be needed if victory was to be achieved.

During the battle around Dak To the fighting at Hill 875 was as violent as any in the war. Members of the 173rd Airborne Brigade crouch down in a shell crater as mortar fire drops around them. Closest man is armed with a CAR-15 (US Army)

Troopers from the 173rd keep low as enemy fire whistles overhead. In the battle for Hill 875 the unit performed so gallantly that they received a Presidential Unit Citation. The entrenched NVA regiment suffered over 800 men killed in the battle for the hill that was finally captured on Thanksgiving Day. (US Army)

1968-A Year Of Decision

By the end of 1967 communist forces throughout Vietnam were in disarray. Many of the Viet Cong and North Vietnamese units had been severely mauled in combat with US forces and most of their base camps had been destroyed. Only in I Corps did the US face a serious military challenge. In the far northwestern corner of I Corps, two full NVA divisions surrounded a marine regiment at Khe Sanh in a possible attempt to inflict a Dien Bien Phu-type of defeat on the Americans. To counter this threat elements from the 1st Cav and the newly arrived 101st Airborne Division were sent to reinforce Khe Sanh.

But while the enemy made it appear they were focusing their attention on this isolated position, a far more ambitious plan was about to be unveiled. By this stage in the war the communists had realized that they could not militarily defeat US forces. However, they sensed that if they could achieve a major propaganda victory the US public, becoming increasingly weary of the war, might clamor for a political solution. Thus, the communist high command decided to unleash a series of suicidal attacks against military and civilian targets. They hoped that these attacks would spark a general uprising of ARVN troops and civilians who would join them in attacks against US forces. Preparations for this assault took place while the battle for Khe Sanh was shaping up. Enemy troops infiltrated into the cities and stockpiled weapons in preparation for the attack. To achieve maximum surprise the communists decided to launch this offensive during the traditional Tet cease-fire* when the vigilance of US and ARVN forces was at its lowest. On the morning of 31 January, the enemy unleashed their long planned attack. Rockets slammed into every major South Vietnamese city, while troops already in position attempted to seize strategic points such as police stations, armories, and airstrips. Outside the cities other units attempted to break through allied lines to link up with guerrillas already in the cities. Perhaps the least significant military effort was the attempt by a small group of infiltrators to storm the US Embassy in Saigon. Yet this got massive coverage in the United States press, press coverage far out of proportion to its significance.

As the first news of the Saigon Embassy attack filtered into the United States, ARVN troops were already moving to counter the enemy assaults. Savage street fighting occurred in Saigon and Hue as allied soldiers fought to root out the entrenched enemy. As the military tide turned against them, the VC and NVA infiltrators carried out a series of mass executions of civilians. In Hue alone over 5000 people were brutally tortured and murdered before the communists were driven out of the city.

In the month of fighting which followed the attack, nearly 1000 American soldiers died while over 4,500 were wounded. But the enemy losses were far in excess of this. Roughly 20,000 VC and NVA died during this period, while 30-40,000 were wounded. And, except for the citadel in Hue they were unable to hold any key points for a prolonged period of time. Militarily this attack was a disaster, yet thanks to the grossly distorted media coverage of it in the press, the communists achieved a propaganda victory without parallel in modern history. In the United States the anti-war movement made political capital of the battle, and more and more people began to question US involvement in the war. One month after the Tet Offensive ended, President Johnson announced he would not run for another term, and began cutting back the aerial bombardment of North Vietnam . What the communist forces could not win on the battlefield they were given by the American press.

However, while the communists were achieving this massive propaganda victory in the United States, their forces in Vietnam were suffering one reversal after another. Once the initial onslaught was over, US and ARVN forces counterattacked the decimated enemy formations. Near Saigon elements of the 1st, 9th, and 25th Infantry Divisions, supported by the 11th Armored Cavalry Regiment and ARVN units, swept the area surrounding the capital in OPERATION QUYET THANG. By the beginning of April over 2600 guerrillas had been killed. In addition large numbers of arms caches were also seized. While this operation was going on, the 1st Cavalry Division and units of the 3rd Marine Division began OPERATION PEGASUS, to relieve the surrounded marines at Khe Sanh. Using helicopters the airborne soldiers leapfrogged over the NVA position to cut off their retreat to Laos. As

*Tet is something like a combination of Christmas and New Years to the Vietnamese.

On the eve of the TET offensive US forces in the field were unaware of what the enemy had in store for the cities throughout Vietnam. These members of the 199th Infantry Brigade look over a map of the area near Bien Hoa during a sweep of the area. Soldier on the right wears one of the low visibility patches which replaced the earlier more colorful ones. (US Army)

the marines pushed to Khe Sanh numerous enemy units were caught in the squeeze. During the two week operation the North Vietnamese lost over 1000 men. The official relief of the base came on 8 April, although PEGASUS was not officially terminated until 15 April.

Air bases were a prime target during the TET offensive. This bunker at Tan Son Nhut was captured early in the attack by the Viet Cong but a combination of American infantry, air force police, and ARVN tanks recaptured it. (USAF)

Four days later the 1st Cav, 101st Airborne, and elements of the 196th Infantry Brigade began OPERATION DELAWARE. This drive was aimed at the A Shau Valley, a communist stronghold southwest of Hue which contained numerous supply depots, base camps, and infiltration routes from Laos. The initial attack involved four helicopter assault into the valley by the 1st Cav while other US and ARVN units drove from the east on the ground. The helicopters were greeted by intense ground fire but were able to land their troops. Following the initial assault the cavalry troops began to fan out in the valley. As the operation progressed, enemy resistance increased. Throughout the remainder of April communist troops fought savagely as they were forced back by US troops. By the end of the month their resistance was broken. Over 850 NVA soldiers died in the month long campaign which ended in mid-May. Huge quantities of arms and supplies that had been painstakingly stockpiled over a two year period were destroyed. These losses in men and material effectively crippled the communists in the region for the remainder of 1968.

As April turned into May the United States and Hanoi announced they were ready to sit down and discuss peace proposals in Paris. One day after this news broke, communists forces launched a series of suicidal attacks across South Vietnam. However, this time surprise was not on their side, and despite some bitter fighting, the attacks were repulsed with huge losses. Because of these heavy losses of men and material this was the last major attack carried out by the communists during 1968. Throughout the remainder of the year the communists had to content themselves with long range rocket and mortar attacks against allied bases and Vietnamese civilian population centers. To counter these terror tactics, the allies carried out numerous sweeps around the cities to destroy arms caches and root out the remaining enemy soldiers. By fall these rocket attacks had subsided considerably and US and ARVN troops were able to switch their sweeps away from the cities and back into the countryside. The depleted enemy forces were sought out and brought to bay whenever possible. Unwilling to stand and fight, those units which were able, fled across the border into sanctuaries in Cambodia and Laos to rest and regroup. By the year's end, few full strength communist formations remained inside Vietnam. What was left consisted mostly of basically local guerrillas who were incapable of seriously hampering US and Vietnamese forces.

(Above Right) This MP jeep was ambushed as it responded to a call for help on the night of the initial enemy attack. All the occupants were killed. (US Army)

(Above Left)The enemy scored a tremendous propaganda victory when a sapper team managed to penetrate the US Embassy compound in Saigon on the first night of the attack. Two MPs from the 716th MP battalion keep a sharp lookout for any VC activity around the embassy while other troops root out the sappers inside. The soldier on the left wears standard jungle boots while the one on the right wears the all leather combat boots. The upper portion of the jungle boot was made of a Green synthetic material. (US Army)

Members of the 1st Infantry Division search a cemetery on the outskirts of Saigon a few days after the start of TET. Prior to the offensive the VC staged a number of fake funerals, burying coffins filled with weapons. These weapons were retrieved just before the attack. (US Army)

A weary machinegunner from the 199th Infantry Brigade surveys the devastation in Cholon, the Chinese quarter of Saigon, after a week of severe fighting. This section of Saigon was almost totally destroyed by a combination of street fighting, artillery bombardment, and air strikes. When the author went through this section four years later, it still bore heavy marks of the vicious fighting. (US Army)

(Above Right) An M-113 from the 25th Infantry Division supports troops of the 1st Infantry Division near a cemetery in Saigon. The vehicle is fitted with an early style armored shield on the commanders hatch and carries sandbags on the deck for additional protection from small arms fire. (US Army)

While most of the fighting during TET took place in the cities, the war still went on in the countryside. A soldier from the Americal Division watches a group of prisoners file past the body of a Viet Cong killed during a sweep through the village. (U.S. Army)

The shoulder insignia is that of the 173rd Airborne Brigade, while the winged insignia on the helmets is from the 82nd Airborne. These troops have just arrived in-country and are awaiting a flight to their new base. (US Army)

Above Right) A soldier from the 1st Cav, carrying an M-72 LAW on his back, watches intently as an engineer prepares to rig a booby trap for demolition. One problem with the M-72 LAW carried by the soldier was its inability to function if moisture got inside the firing mechanism. A fair percentage of them failed because of this problem. (US Army)

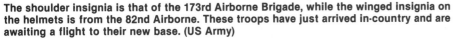

M-79 Grenade Launcher

A grenadier from the 9th Infantry Division prepares to fire a grenade at a suspected enemy position in a tree line. The M-79 covered the area between the longest distance of the handthrown grenade and the shortest distance of the mortar. As such it was an excellent infantry weapon. (US Army)

The Riverine forces evolved their own tactics to compensate for the vast tracts of water they had to operate over. This landing craft has been fitted with a special deck to allow helicopters to land on it. These craft were often used as makeshift hospitals until wounded could be flown to better facilities. (US Army)

(Right) A squad leader and his sergeant take a break during operations in Binh Hoa province. The lieutenant in the background is armed with a CAR-15 while the sergeant has a newer M-16 with a forward assist to ram home any round which may get stuck in the chamber. (US Army)

Jungle Uniforms

Exposed Buttons

Covered Buttons

Combat Boot

Jungle Boot

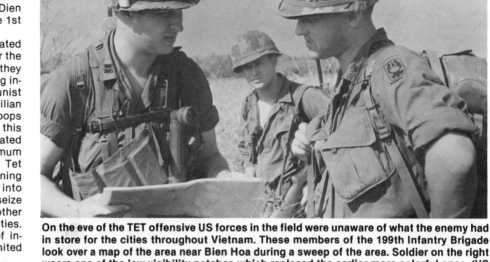

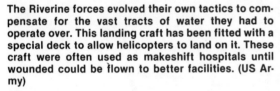

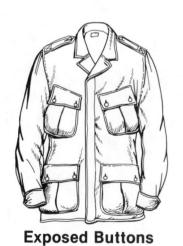

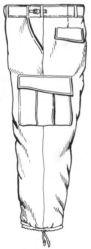

Exposed Buttons

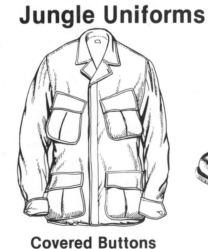

Covered Buttons

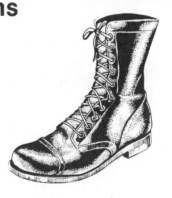

Combat Boot

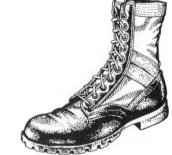

Jungle Boot

CAR-15 Rifle

This soldier gingerly moves over a tree-trunk bridge in the Mekong Delta.

(Above Left) Many attempts were made to provide the troops with better transportation in the delta area. This airboat, similar to ones used in Florida, is manned by soldiers from the 199th Infantry Brigade. They are taking part in a sweep through Gia Dinh province south of Saigon. (US Army)

In an attempt to combine the M-16 and M-79 into one weapon the XM148 was developed. However, it was felt that the performance of the M-79 was superior and this weapon did not gain widespread use. (US Army/Author)

(Above Right) A member of the Americal Division fires at a suspected VC position near Chu Lai as an M-113 stands ready to give support if needed. The Americal Division was the only unit of division size to be formed within Vietnam during the war. (US Army)

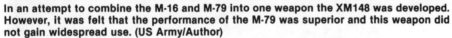

M-148
(M-16/M-79)

A dog handler and his German Shepherd rest during a patrol with elements of the 25th Infantry Division near Fire Support Base Wire. Dog teams trained together and if the handler was rotated home or wounded, the dog was not reassigned to another handler but put into different duties such as security. (US Army)

Vietnamization and Redeployment

The beginning of 1969 saw a new US President, Richard M Nixon, take office. One of his campaign pledges had been to hand the ground war back to the South Vietnamese. During the early part of the year little was done about this promise, US troops continued to operate in the field against the communists. However, the level of activity was extremely low when compared to the previous year. By the spring Nixon felt the time ripe to announce a major troop withdrawal of 25,000 men, to be completed by the end of August. Besides various logistic troops two brigades of the 9th Infantry Division were slated for this withdrawal.

Unfortunately the communists took advantage of this gesture to launch a series of attacks from their border sanctuaries in Cambodia. Units of the 1st Cav and the 11th Armored Cavalry Regiment were subjected to massive ground assaults but repulsed the enemy with heavy losses. In September, following the death of Ho Chi Minh, the North Vietnamese stepped up their activity north of Saigon. Most of these attacks were little more then quick forays from Cambodia with the intent of inflicting as many allied casualties as possible. Gone were the days when the communists could keep large units inside Vietnam. Most of the major fighting now centered around the border regions.

With this in mind, President Nixon felt it was safe to order more troops home, despite this upsurge of fighting. During the fall of 1969 US forces in the Mekong Delta turned over their responsibilities to ARVN units. An additional 40,000 men were rotated home by the end of the year, including the single brigade of the 82nd Airborne Division which had been deployed to Vietnam. As the level of fighting dropped off, those US forces which remained saw a substantial decrease in casualties.

The Cambodian Invasion

By the beginning of 1970 the enemy within Vietnam had been defeated. Scattered bands of Viet Cong and North Vietnamese still operated inside the country, but they posed no serious military threat to US or ARVN forces. American forces had been reduced from over 530,000 in 1968 to just under 340,000 by January 1970. During the first part of 1970 another 40,000 men were redeployed home, including the 1st Infantry Division and a brigade from the 4th Infantry Division. Even as these troop withdrawals were taking place, however, a serious problem still faced the United States. Even though the communists had been militarily defeated within Vietnam, they still had sizeable numbers of troops in various sanctuaries across the border in Cambodia and Laos. Although the US military command had often requested permission to clear these sanctuaries out, previous administrations had refused since this would have involved the invasion of a supposedly "neutral" country. Yet it seemed alright for the communists to occupy parts of these neutral countries and attack US and ARVN forces. Fortunately President Nixon realized the absurdity of the situation and decided that unless these sanctuaries were cleared the whole process of Vietnamization would be jeapordized. In the late spring of 1970, Nixon gave the order to move on the sanctuaries in Cambodia.

The initial thrusts into Cambodia were made by ARVN forces in mid-April. On 1 May the 1st Cavalry Division made an airmobile assault into the "Fishhook", a deep, narrow projection into Vietnam near Loc Ninh. At the same time elements of the 11th Armored Cavalry Regiment carried out a ground attack to link up with the airborne soldiers and destroy any enemy units or base camps caught in this pincer move. To the south of this drive, a brigade task force from the 25th Infantry Division hit hard at enemy troops north of Tay Ninh as they drove toward the Cambodian towns of Krek and Memot. Further north the 4th Infantry Division, in conjunction with ARVN forces, pushed into Cambodia from Pleiku and seized a hugh North Vietnamese base camp.

During the first week of the invasion over 1000 of the enemy perished in the "Fishhook" alone. Nearly 4,800 individual or crew served weapons, 100 trucks, 40,000 pounds of explosives, and a million rounds of ammunition were seized in the drive. On May 7th the invasion was expanded when the 3rd Brigade of the 9th Infantry Division struck the "Parrot's Beak", a curved projection which jutted into Vietnam to the south of Tay Ninh. As this drive got underway troops from the 1st Cav in the "Fishhook" uncovered a vast, sprawling complex of huts, bunkers, and supplies which encompassed over two square miles. This was nicknamed the "City", and as the complex was searched more material was uncovered, including a swimming pool.

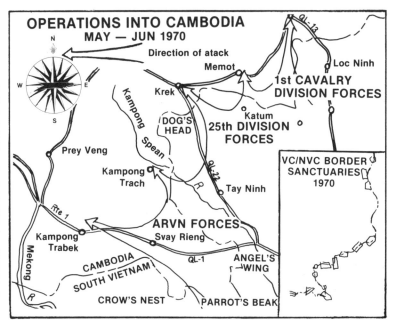

A road patrol from the 173rd Airborne Brigade fires at a group of Viet Cong who tried to ambush them. Firing the .50 caliber machinegun exposed the gunner to return fire and most gunners wore a flak jacket for protection. The soldier's camouflage fatigues were not standard issue to infantry units and were probably bought from a Vietnamese store or on the black market. (US Army)

With the start of the second week of operations a joint US and Vietnamese Riverine force, supported by the 9th Infantry Division, sailed up the Mekong River into Cambodia. Their object was the 88th North Vietnamese Regiment which threatened the Cambodian capital of Phnom Penh. Eventually ARVN units pushed on to an area near the Phnom Penh while US forces covered their flanks. In the other areas of the invasion this also became the standard practice as Nixon, in response to anti-war critics, decreed that US forces would only move approximately twenty-five miles into Cambodia. As opposition to this invasion grew in intensity in the United States, he further announced that all American forces would be withdrawn from Cambodia by the end of June. Thus, the communists withdrew as many of their units as possible beyond the twenty-five mile limit in and effort to wait out the US drive. New attacks were made to cut off as many of the retreating VC and NVA as possible before they got beyond the twenty-five mile restriction. Unfortunately, most of the enemy were able to evade these sweeps, but in their retreat they abandoned vast quantities of materials. By the middle of June the number of contacts dropped off dramatically and US troops spent the rest of the month removing or destroying the munitions and supplies they had captured. In accordance wih Nixon's directive the last troops pulled out of Cambodia on 30 June.

During the two month operation American casualties were 337 killed and 1524 wounded. Over 11,000 enemy soliders perished during this period, and their material losses set the communists back over a year in terms of mounting any sizeable offensive operations against South Vietnam. In the future, ARVN forces would return to disrupt attempts to re-establish base camps or supply lines in these areas, but these attacks would be without the help of US troops. It was felt that the South Vietnamese forces were now strong enough to keep these sanctuaries cleared without American troops.

Withdrawal

Following the Cambodian Invasion US troop redeployment increased sharply. From the end of the invasion to December, 1970, units from the 4th, 9th and 25th Infantry Divisions, plus the 199th Infantry Brigade, were withdrawn from Vietnam. These troop cuts dropped American strength to 250,000 men by the beginning of 1971, as troop strength dropped more and more of the fighting was shifted to ARVN forces. The only large scale ground operation that involved US forces was JEFFERSON GLENN, which was carried out with the ARVN 1st Infantry Division near Hue. Otherwise, the fighting slackened as American forces took up a more defensive posture throughout Vietnam.

During 1971 the bulk of US combat units were sent home. By year's end only the 3rd Brigade from the 1st Cav, the 196th Infantry Brigade, a few infantry battalions, and some cavalry squadrons remained in-country. To highlight this, President Nixon stipulated in November that U.S. troops were no longer to participate in offensive missions. Prior to this the last large scale operation by American troops took place near the old marine base at Khe Sanh. The 1st Brigade of the 5th Infantry Division began DEWEY CANYON II at the end of January to establish a base for the South Vietnamese incursion into Laos. This was the last major US ground action of the war. After the ARVN troops withdrew from Laos, the base was abandoned and the brigade pulled back to Quang Tre.

In 1972 all ground forces were withdrawn, despite North Vietnam's invasion during the spring. Only advisors and a few helicopter units still remained inside Vietnam. The war had come full circle. With the aid of airpower the South Vietnamese were able to stop the NVA drive. Finally, after a massive aerial assault on Hanoi the communist leaders agreed to a cease fire at the beginning of 1973. Despite this cease fire fighting continued between the communist forces and the South Vietnamese. In the two years which followed, the NVA forces grew stronger while ARVN declined in strength. During the spring of 1975 the NVA launched an all out drive to capture South Vietnam. Without US support South Vietnamese units fell apart. With communist forces on the outskirts of Saigon, Marines were sent in to protect the evacuation of all remaining American personnel. On 29 April, 1975 enemy rockets slammed into Tan Son Nhut airbase, killing two marines. These were the last U.S. servicemen to die in Vietnam. The next day, all Americans left Vietnam.

The war was over.

A patrol from the 4th Infantry Division makes final preparations before moving out from LZ Valentine. The value of the vegetation in the helmet band is questionable and was not often used by American troops. (US Army)

Streams were crossed in any way possible. Here a soldier from the 199th Infantry Brigade uses an air mattress to support his gear as he pulls himself across the stream on a rope stretches between the two banks. Although a good means of cooling off, this type of crossing exposed the soldier to a host of waterborne parasites that could cause serious infections and illness. (US Army)

A heavily laden machinegunner trudges up a hill near Pleiku. With all his gear, M-60, and ammunition he is probably carrying around eighty pounds of weight. It is easy to see how this could sap a mans strength, especially in the hot, hilly terrain of the Central Highlands. Although the belts of ammunition provide a quick means of ready access, their Brass color reflected in the sunlight and gave the enemy a few extra minutes of warning to set up an ambush or escape. (US Army)

A company commander radios in the discovery of a bunker complex to his battalion while other members watch for possible enemy snipers. The jungle fatigues proved very practical in the hot climate. Most of the men are wearing a towel around their necks. (US Army)

A group of American and ARVN soldiers interrogate a captured Viet Cong during a sweep by the Americal Division near Chu Lai in the summer of 1969. (US Army)

(Above Left) As the war progressed more and more soldiers became "hippy" and took to wearing beads and colorful scarves. Though this may have been a psychological boost for their moral, its affect on camouflage and concealment was counterproductive. (US Army)

FRONT TOWARD ENEMY

Claymore Anti-Personnel Mine

A soldier checks out cooking utensils for possible booby traps on Berri Island off the coast near Chu Lai. The ace of spades in his helmet was the card of death to the Vietnamese and many troops carried them as a psychological means of frightening the locals. (US Army)

As the process of Vietnamization took effect more and more emphasis was placed on fixed defenses to protect US forces. These bunkers are part of the main line of defense around an artillery base near Phu Bai. The wire fence in front will hopefully detonate any rocket propelled grenades (RPGs) which the Viet Cong or North Vietnamese might fire. (US Army)

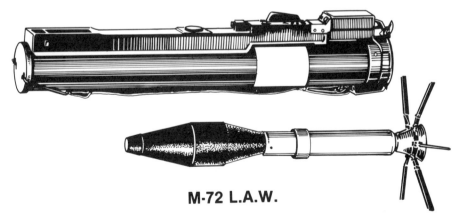

M-72 L.A.W.

Helmet graffiti became very common as the war progressed. This photo shows one which obviously belongs to a chaplain. Most graffiti on the helmets was not repeatable in polite company. (US Army)

41

Mud was a constant companion in the Mekong Delta. This soldier from the 9th Infantry Division tries to clean some of it off after a firefight with a group of Viet Cong. His M-16 will be one of the first things cleaned up since the weapon was seldom able to function in such a state. (US Army)

A "tunnel rat" lowers himself into the entrance of a Viet Cong complex near Bien Hoa. In such confined space a pistol was far more suitable than a rifle. The gas mask helped protect him from gas or smoke which may have been pumped into the tunnel. (US Army)

A platoon leader calls in an air strike during a search mission northwest of Lai Khe by the 1st Infantry Division. The small bottles in the helmet bands of the RTO and his backup are insect repellent and oil for their M-16s. (US Army)

(Above Right) Evacuating the wounded was always difficult, especially in the swampy terrain of the Mekong Delta or the coastal regions in I Corps. This soldier is being carried out of the jungle by his comrades from the 101st Airborne after an ambush by NVA troops. Such conditions made it very easy for a wound to become seriously infected. (US Army)

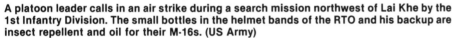

**M-67 90mm
Recoiless Rifle**

As the war began to wind down, US troops took more of a role in programs to win the people over to the South Vietnamese government. These soldiers from the 25th Infantry Division are providing protection for a medical team which is treating the people of a small village near An Duc. (US Army)

43

Members of the 199th Infantry Brigade descend through rocky ground to a stream bed during operations north of Saigon. The terrain in Vietnam was not just lush, tropical jungle or wet marshland. (Chernak/Seitz)

(Above Left) These soldiers are looking over the wreckage of a Huey that was shot down as it came into a "hot" LZ. Other troops watch for evidence of enemy activity as another helicopter approaches to bring in supplies and evacuate wounded. (Chernak/Seitz)

Men from the 25th Infantry Division follow a tank during an operation north of Tay Ninh in the middle of February, 1970. Although it was easier to follow the path made by an armored vehicle, any element of surprise was lost, which often allowed the enemy to either slip away or spring an ambush. The closest soldier is carrying an M-67 90mm recoilless rifle which proved very effective in destroying bunkers. (US Army)

A medic from the 199th treats a minor wound in the field. Each unit had a number of corpsmen to handle casualties during the initial stages of a battle. Many acts of heroism were performed by these medics who were a prime target for enemy snipers. Often an American soldier was only wounded because the enemy knew a medic would try to get to the injured man, giving them the opportunity to pick the medic off. (Chernak/Seitz)

A patrol takes a break during a sweep near Fire Support Base "Libby" located approximately forty miles northeast of Saigon. Extra canteens are carried by the RTO. (Chernak/Seitz)

45

Members of the 173rd Airborne Brigade return enemy sniper fire while on a search mission north of the Ai Lao river near Bong Song. Enemy snipers were often so well camouflaged that the only way to kill them was by spraying the sniper's suspected area location with fire. (US Army)

(Right) A machinegunner from the 199th Infantry Brigade lays down a field of fire to provide cover during a helicopter assault into a "hot" LZ near Xuan Loc. A machinegunner was supported by an ammo bearer and sometimes another man to provide security in case of an enemy attack. Xuan Loc was the site of the final ARVN defeat five years later, during the spring of 1975. (Chernak/Seitz)

The major event during 1970 was the invasion of Cambodia which involved a combined helicopter and armored assault on enemy border sanctuaries. These M-113 APCs move into the Cambodian town of Snoul which was a vital center of logistics for the communist forces. (US Army)

These troops pause to survey an area before moving on. The officer (foreground) holds a CAR-15. Ammunition and water were two of the most necessary items needed by troops in the field. The standing troopers have at least nine extra magazines of ammunition visible and they probably have more on their backs. Most soldiers carried as much ammunition as possible. (US Army)

(Above Right) A captain from the 199th questions a villager during a search. The shaving brush in his helmet is for cleaning the CAR-15 hanging on his shoulder. The shoulder patch is the low visibility type.

Members of a scout dog unit search an enemy training center inside Cambodia. They are from the 25th Infantry Division which was responsibile for the "Fishhook", an area to the west of Loc Ninh. The dog handler has a thirty round magazine in his M-16 which was rather uncommon. (US Army)

A look of obvious weariness is on the face of this grunt as he pauses during an ambush patrol. On such missions the men rarely carried heavy packs or wore steel helmets, both encumbered them which could prove fatal on an ambush mission. (US Army)

(Above Left) A huge amount of supplies and munitions were uncovered in the sweeps through the border sanctuaries. Members of the 25th Infantry Division examine ammunition and explosives which were captured near Snoul. The material will either be destroyed or removed by helicopters to Vietnam. (US Army)

A platoon leader tells his RTO to notify the company that they have uncovered a VC camp. Note the various smoke and hand grenades carried by each man plus the K bar carried on the back of the radio. (US Army)

These soldiers await the final journey home to their loved ones. Over 55,000 Americans died in Vietnam and surrounding countries and many of their bodies passed through this mortuary warehouse on the outskirts of Tan Son Nhut. If more of the politicians had visited this place they might have been willing to wage a war rather than playing politics with men's lives. (US Army)

Even though the Vietnam war has been over for many years reports persist that American servicemen are still being held as prisoners in Vietnam. Let us do all we can to insure that, if this is indeed true, every effort is made to get these brave men back. The people of the United States owe them that.

US ELITE FORCES
-VIETNAM

squadron/signal publications

(Right) In the Mekong Delta during August of 1967, a US Navy SEAL provides suppressive fire with his Stoner M63A1 LMG.

(Left and Below) Members of the 1st Force Recon Company prepare to eliminate a Viet Cong 'tax collector' at long range during February of 1967. The Recon, who is standing, both spots for the sniper and provides close-range security for both of them with his M3A1 .45 caliber SMG.

(Below) Two US Navy SEALs come ashore on a raid ing April of 1970. The SEAL in the water is armed with M63A1 Stoner fitted with a 150 round drum maga The SEAL jumping from the boat carries an M-16 e ped with a M203 grenade launcher, grenades for are carried in the special combat vest he wears.

(Right) During January of 1966 a Marine of the 3rd Recon Battalion marks sites of possible enemy arms caches as he observes a hamlet from hiding. He uses his camouflage helmet cover as headgear and wears World War II pattern camouflage. His K-Bar knife holds his map down.

US ELITE FORCES
-VIETNAM

By Leroy Thompson

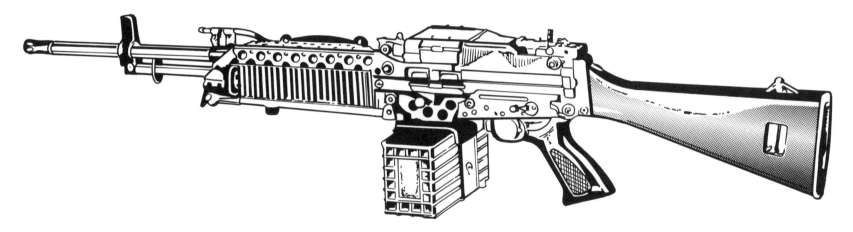

Color Illustrations by Ken MacSwan
illustrated by Kevin Wornkey

 **squadron/signal publications**

Prior to rescuing ARVN POWs in the Mekong Delta a US Navy SEAL prepares to silently eliminate a Viet Cong sentry using a Smith & Wesson Mark 22, Model O silenced 9ᴍᴍ 'Hush Puppy' pistol.

If you have any photographs of the aircraft, armor, soldiers or ships of any nation, particularly wartime snapshots, why not share them with us and help make Squadron/Signal's books all the more interesting and complete in the future. Any photograph sent to us will be copied and the original returned. The donor will be fully credited for any photos used. Please indicate if you wish us not to return the photos. Please send them to: Squadron/Signal Publications, Inc., 1115 Crowley Dr., Carrollton, TX 75011-5010.

Special Forces Beret Badge

During October of 1968 Navy a SEAL waits in ambush along a trail in the Mekong Delta. He wears faded locally made tiger stripes trousers. The Olive Drab head scarf and the M63A1 5.56ᴍᴍ Stoner light machine gun are both typical of SEALs. (US Navy)

INTRODUCTION

WHITE STAR and Other Early Training Missions

There seems to be something in the American character or way of life that views the very existence of elite armed forces with a great deal of suspicion. And while elite forces are used during a time of war, and indeed often glorified by the media their very existence is underlined in controversy. Both in and out of the military there is constant criticism, and indeed even pressure to dissolve any organization considered to be an elite force within any of the branches of service. Regardless of how this controversy is resolved in the future, if ever, the elite forces did an extraordinary job in the past and can be counted on to do so in the future, when need rears its ugly head.

The peculiar nature and circumstances of the Vietnam War were such that it provided fertile ground for the growth of elite forces and the development of *special mission* tactics especially the Army's Special Forces. However, each branch of service had an elite special mission trained organization and the Army and Air Force had more than one:

Army	— Special Forces
Army	— Rangers
Army	— Long Range Reconnaissance Patrols
Navy	— SEALs
Marines	— Recons
Air Force	— Combat Control Teams
Air Force	— Combat Security Police

The Army's Special Forces, the largest and perhaps consequently the most controversial of all the American Elite troops can serve as a focus to introducing one to the elite troops belonging to the other branches of service. This is especially so since much of the tactics and training were pioneered and developed by the men of the Special Forces — the Green Berets.

During World War II the Office of Strategic Services (OSS) — the conceptual forerunner of American Special Forces — was active in Southeast Asia. However, the involvement of US Special Forces in Southeast Asia is traced to 1954 when a team from the 77th Special Forces Group (Airborne) was sent to Thailand to train Royal Thai Rangers. During the next few years members of the 14th Special Forces Detachment from Hawaii saw limited service in Vietnam and Thailand as trainers. Small training missions continued into the late 1950s when the 1st Special Forces Group (Airborne) sent personnel to South Vietnam from Okinawa. The South Vietnamese Special Forces were founded when the Joint Observation Battalion evolved into the ARVN 31st and 77th Special Forces Battalions in 1959. Members of the US Army Special Forces were involved in training these early Vietnamese special mission troops. A 77th SFG (Abn) team was also involved in founding and training the *Biet Dong Quan* (South Vietnamese Rangers) during this time period. In May of 1960 thirty US Special Forces instructors from Fort Bragg were sent to the Republic of Vietnam as a training cadre.

An important event for Special Forces involved in Southeast Asia had happened earlier in neighboring Laos. During the summer of 1959, LT COL 'Bull' Simons, later to win fame as the leader of the Son Tay POW Raid, took FC-3, which consisted of 107 members of the Army's Special Forces into Laos to train the Laotian Army in counterinsurgency tactics. Known as WHITE STAR this mobile training team initially operated in civilian clothes and *theoretically* operated clandestinely. However, in reality there was little secrecy about their presence or their mission since on their arrival Radio Hanoi had, in fact, welcomed them over the airwaves. By 1961 OPERATION WHITE STAR had grown to 300-400 troopers operating in US uniforms.

Perhaps the most important development resulting from WHITE STAR was the training of Meo hill tribesmen as counterinsurgency forces. Normally operating in half A-Teams (normally six men, but sometimes seven), members of the Special Forces trained the Meos into the most effective anti-Communist force in Laos. Under General Vang Pao the

In December of 1962 two members of Detachment A-14 inspect the punji stakes imbedded in a trench around the hamlet of Chau-Lang as part of its defenses. The trooper on the right carries a M1A1 Carbine. (US Army)

Meos would continue as the most reliable counter to the Pathet Lao for many years. In southern Laos the Kha were also organized into light infantry counterinsurgency forces and trained by Special Forces. These indigenous Laotian strike forces were the fore-runners of similar units which the Special Forces would raise and train under the Civilian Irregular Defense Group (CIDG) program in Vietnam.

Theoretically, the US Army Special Forces was pulled out of Laos in October of 1962, as a result of an agreement reached in July of 1962 that all foreign military personnel would leave Laos. However, since the North Vietnamese Army (NVA) was blatantly ignoring the agreement, only a portion of the Special Forces personnel left. Many just headed for the Chu Porn Mountains and continued to work with General Vang Pao's Meos. Others went back to civilian clothes and worked in Laos on assignment to the CIA. At various times during the 1950s and early 1960s, Special Forces advisors in Laos and Vietnam ended up in civilian clothes as members of the Programs Evaluation Office in Laos or the Combined Studies Group in Vietnam. Either of these euphemisms could have been abbreviated CIA. While theoretically there as advisors and trainers only, members of Special Forces went on combat operations whenever possible. In February of 1962 for example, Special Forces personnel jumped into combat at Nam Tah along with the Royal Laotian 55th Parachute Battalion.

While they would not be deployed to Vietnam as a group until August of 1964, another important early landmark for Special Forces in Vietnam was the activation on 21 September 1961 of the 5th Special Forces Group (Airborne) at Fort Bragg. This early experience in Southeast Asia, especially the success of WHITE STAR with the Meos and Kha, and the establishment of the 5th Special Forces Group (Airborne) set the stage for the later intense Special Forces effort in the Republic of Vietnam.

Special Forces Training and Organization

To understand Special Forces missions and methods of operation, it is useful to have some knowledge of US Special Forces training and organization. Before undergoing Special Forces selection a soldier had to already be airborne qualified, and in many cases he was also Ranger qualified. Upon selection for Special Forces training he would receive intensive schooling in one of the following specialties:

COMMUNICATIONS: Sixteen weeks of training during which the trainee learned to send and receive Morse Code at a minimum rate of eighteen words per minute, cryptograhic skills, and the operation, repair, and maintenance of transmitting and receiving equipment, generators, and antennas.

MEDICAL: Thirty-seven to fifty weeks of Medical training during which skills through emergency field surgery and dentistry were learned. In addition to providing basic medical care to indigenous troops, their families, and members of his A-detachment, the Special Forces medic was also trained to teach hygiene and disease prevention.

DEMOLITIONS AND ENGINEERING: Eight weeks of training in demolitions and construction. Demolitions training placed special emphasis on creating explosives from available materials and the use of explosives for special tasks. Incendiaries, mines, and booby traps were also studied. Construction skills included dam, bridge, well and stockade building intended to aid in civic action programs.

Members of the US Special Forces inspect the remains of the village of Nam Qui during December of 1962. The large jars on the right were used in preparing *Nuoc-man*, the fish paste no Special Forces veteran will ever forget. (US Army)

WEAPONS: Eight weeks of training in both US and foreign weapons. About one third of the training was spent on mortars and another third on machine guns, rifles, carbines, and shotguns. The remainder of the time was spent on submachineguns, handguns, anti-tank weapons, grenade launchers, grenades, tactical training, building field ranges, and marksmanship training methods.

OPERATIONS AND INTELLIGENCE: Eight weeks of training covering tactical terrain, analysis, fingerprinting, order of battle, operational planning, photography, cryptography, clandestine communications, intelligence nets, methods of interrogation, organizing guerrilla units, and psychological warfare.

All specialties received training in techniques of teaching their skills. Normally, each man received cross training in at least one other specialty, thus allowing more flexibility should a member of a team be injured or the team be split.

The basic Special Forces operational unit was the A-detachment consisting of twelve men and was designed so it could be split into two six man 1/2 A-Detachments because of the duplication of skills within the A-Detachment. The A-Detachment was organized as follows:

Commanding Officer (captain)
Executive Officer (lieutenant)
Operations Sergeant (E8)
Heavy Weapons Leader (E7)
Intelligence Sergeant or Assistant Operations Sergeant (E7)
Light Weapons Leader (E7)
Medical Specialist (E7)
Radio Operator Supervisor (E7)
Engineer Sergeant (E7)
Assistant Medical Specialist (E6)
Chief of Research and Development Operator or Radio Operator (E5)
Engineer (E5)

The Civilian Irregular Defense Group (CIDG) Program

The success in training minorities in Laos, coupled with the need to deprive the Viet Cong (VC) free access to critical hamlets in the Central Highlands of South Vietnam convinced US and Vietnamese authorities of the advantages of implementing a local defense plan among the Montagnard tribesmen during the Fall of 1961. The *Yards* had traditionally been looked down upon by the Vietnamese who referred to them as *moi* which meant savages. The Montagnards were ready targets for the Communists who attempted to play upon both their distrust of the Vietnamese and their fear of the Viet Cong (VC).

To counter VC incursions, the *Rhade* (most prevalent Montagnard tribe) village of *Buon Enao* and its surrounding hamlets in *Darlac* Province were selected for a pilot Village Defense Program, which would evolve into the Civilian Irregular Defense Group (CIDG) effort. To help in civic action, primarily medical and engineering, a 1/2 A-Detachment of US Special Forces and some Vietnamese Special Forces — the *Luc Luong Dac Biet* (LLDB) — were first deployed to *Buon Enao* during December of 1961. This LLDB detachment contained a substantial number of Montagnards to help counter the Montagnard distrust of the Army of the Republic of Vietnam (ARVN).

By February of 1962, an A-team from the 1st Special Forces Group (airborne) along with an LLDB team had arrived to train these local Defense Forces in basic military skills and to help the villages establish defenses. In addition to small arms usage — primarily the M1 Carbine and M3 'Grease Gun' — building stockades and trenches for defense and basic defensive tactics were taught. At least one or two men in each village were given basic instructions in the use of a radio so they could call for assistance during an attack. A central 'strike force' received additional training and was more heavily armed, though it still functioned as irregular light infantry. This 'strike force' was a paid full-time unit which was available to react to attacks upon any village in their area.

By April of 1962, twenty-eight villages were protected by 1,000 village irregular defenders and a 300 man strike force. This number was soon raised to forty villages surrounding *Buon Enao*, and by August of 1962 some 200 villages in *Darlac* Province in the program with five US Special Forces A-Detachments assigned to training and civic action. Special Forces medics were especially effective since the Montagnards badly needed health care.

The program's effectiveness was soon tested at the villages of *Buon Tong Sing* and *Buon Hra Ea Hning* which suffered VC night attacks that were held and then driven off. By the end of 1962 *Darlac* Province was declared secure.

Because of the increasing number of Special Forces detachments being deployed to Vietnam; Headquarters, US Army Special Forces (Provisional) Vietnam was activated in September of 1962. Personnel from the 1st, 5th, and 7th Special Forces Groups were assigned for six month temporary tours of duty (TDY). So fast had the Special Forces commitment grown, primarily because of the CIDG Program, that by November of 1962, there were twenty-six A-Detachments in Vietnam controlled by three B-Detachments, and one C-Detachment.

B-Detachment

In 1964, for approximately each eleven A-Detachments in South Vietnam there was a B-Detachment to provide support to the A-Detachments. However, as the war progressed the ratio of B-Detachments to A-Detachments increased toward a theoretical norm of a B-Detachment for each four A-Detachments. Normally, a B-Detachment consisted of twenty-four men — six officers and eighteen NCOs — and was usually commanded by a Major. In addition to the normal specialties found in an A-Detachment, a B-Detachment included a supply officer and supply sergeant, an intelligence officer, and a preventive medicine specialist. An operational clerk was also assigned, though he was normally a fully-qualified Special Forces soldier who happened to have typing skills.

Members of Special Forces Detachment A-14 supervise construction of defenses at the hamlet of *Chau-Lang* during December of 1962. (US Army)

C-Detachment

A group of B-detachments was controlled by a C-Detachment, sometimes known as a Special Forces company. The C-Detachment normally had a strength of nineteen men — six officers and thirteen NCOs — and was commanded by a Lieutenant Colonel. In addition to the normal specialties represented in the A- and B-Detachments, a C-Detachment included a field radio repairman. Once the 5th Special Forces Group (Airborne) was activated, the theoretical organization was five C-detachments in the Group (one in each corps tactical zone and one assigned directly to the Group commander for special missions) with three B-Detachments to each C-Detachment and four A-Detachments assigned to each B-Detachment. Certain B-Detachments were assigned directly to special operations such as PROJECT DELTA or to training missions such as the LLDB training center.

The continued success of the CIDG Program made its continued expansion desirable. By the end of 1963 US and Vietnamese Special Forces had trained some 18,000 strike force members and more than 43,000 hamlet militia members. Beginning in November of 1962, and continuing through July of 1963, Military Assistance Command Vietnam (MACV)

(Above) Special Forces personnel and *cidgees* during an operation in November of 1965, which resulted in the capture of ten tons of VC explosives. (US Army)

(Above Left) An engineer of Detachment A-14 supervises the cutting of timber for construction of defenses at the hamlet of Chau-Lang in December of 1962. (US Army)

M3A1 "Grease Gun"

(Left) During November of 1965 CIDG personnel and their US Special Forces advisors examine captured explosives found in the hut in the background. (US Army)

7

Special Forces personnel of Detachment A-120 lead their CIDG troops back to *Vinh Khanh* after a two day patrol in the Mountains of II Corps during February of 1966. (US Army)

Special Forces medic of Detachment A-244 checks the wounds of a Montagnard woman rescued during OPERATION HAWTHORNE in June of 1966. Special Forces medics were trained specialists capable of providing a full range of medical services including surgery. (US Army)

Special Forces sergeant of Detachment A-412 at *Cai Cai* uses a Collins single side band radio to maintain contact with a patrol in VC controlled portions of IV Corps during May of 1966. The 'duck hunter' camo outfit worn by this Special Forces sergeant was widely used by CIDG troops during the early 1960s. (US Army)

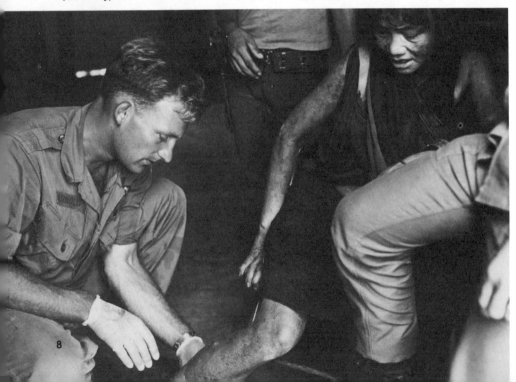

assumed responsibility for the CIDG Program as part of OPERATION SWITCHBACK. During this period, training for strike force troops was standardized at six weeks and for hamlet militia at two weeks.

The thrust of the CIDG Program began to subtly shift during 1963. CIDG strike forces began to patrol aggressively, searching out or setting ambushes for the VC rather than passively waiting for an attack before responding. In October of 1963 the Border Surveillance Program, which had started as the Trail Watcher Program, came under control of the Civilian Irregular Defense Group (CIDG). The Border Surveillance Program made use of Special Forces trained irregulars to watch key Communist infiltration routes along the borders of South Vietnam. This was one of the first examples of a change in concept for the CIDG Program. At about the same time, the Mountain Commandos, another irregular special mission unit, became the Mountain Scouts. Originally, the irregulars had been trained to protect their own villages, but as the program evolved into the later Special Forces fighting camps, encampments were established with military consideration in mind to control key areas.

By 1964 the area development aspects of the CIDG Program had taken a definite secondary role to the establishment of camps as fighting bases from which Special Forces-trained and-led strike forces could carry out offensive operations against the VC. As the CIDG Program expanded it was necessary to establish *strategic hamlets* in areas populated by other ethnic or religious minorities. In III Corps near the Cambodian border the *Khmer Serei* and *Khmer Kampuchea Krom*, among other groups, served in strike forces. The *Hoa Hao* and *Cao Dai* religious sects also furnished strikers, at least a few of whom had served in commandos under the French. The *Nungs*, ethnic Chinese, were also recruited into strike forces, often serving as camp security personnel as well for Special Forces compounds, an indication of their reliability.

During late summer of 1966 General Harold K Johnson, Chief of Staff of the Army, addressed headquarters personnel of the 5th Special Forces Group (Airborne). Standing at the far left is Colonel Francis Kelly, CO of the 5th SFG(Abn). (US Army)

Weapons specialists of the 5th Special Forces Group (Abn) fire an 81мм mortar at Nha Trang during October of 1966. (US Army)

An American Special Forces advisor of Detachment A-301 on patrol with members of the 324th CIDG Company twelve klicks north of *Tay Ninh* City in November of 1966. (US Army)

The traditional animosity between the minorities - especially between the Montagnards — and the Vietnamese often led to problems as CIDG units were turned over to Vietnamese control. At *Buon Enao* and elsewhere, the Vietnamese antagonized the strike forces and the hamlet militias, eventually leading to a rebellion by the Montagnards in September of 1964. Fortunately the US Special Forces — especially such officers as Capt Vernon Gillespie and Maj Edwin Brooks — managed to defuse the rebellion at many camps through the trust they had gained from the Montagnards, but not before some members of the LLDB had been killed or injured by the rebellious *Yards*.

Beginning in November of 1963, and continuing through 1964 priority was given to establishing CIDG camps along the Cambodian and Laotian borders where they could exert control over possible infiltration routes. By 1 July 1964 eighteen Special Forces A-Detachments and 11,250 strike force troops were committed to border surveillance. Throughout 1964 the need for strikers to garrison these border camps virtually eliminated the training of hamlet militia. The burgeoning Special Forces commitment in Vietnam necessitated the presence of a Special Forces Group by 1964, and in October of that year, the 5th Special Forces Group (Airborne) arrived to take control of Special Forces activities in Vietnam. At that time only ninety-five men were assigned to the 5th Special Forces Group.

In addition to conflicts arising from the turnover of CIDG camps to the Vietnamese LLDB, there were also conflicts resulting from the lack of aggressiveness on the part of the LLDB who did not want to go on night ambushes or patrols and did not like to operate with small CIDG units. As a result, while the Vietnamese Special Forces were theoretically in command with US Special Forces troopers along as *advisers*, these American *advisors* often ended up in command. In fact, it was not uncommon for a Special Forces sergeant to find himself in functional command of a unit large enough to be commanded by a captain.

Member of Special Forces Detachment A-321 and members of the LLDB plan a night ambush during OPERATION ATTLEBORO in November of 1966. The US advisor wears tiger stripes camouflage utilities. The scarves they are wearing were worn by many CIDG units in Red, Blue, Green, etc to distinguish units. (US Army)

(Above) A Special Forces demolitions expert prepares C-4 explosive for training purposes at the Tran Sup CIDG training center located six klicks northwest of *Tay Ninh* City. (US Army)

Special Forces Knife

Believed to have been made in Okinawa and issued to Special Forces in Vietnam. It had a 6 3/16' Blue blade and leather washer handle. The cast iron guard and butt is held with a brass nut. The scabbard is made of Black leather.

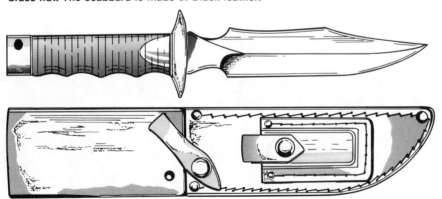

(Right) In November of 1966 members of III Corps MIKE Force, composed of *Nung* Chinese are being extracted by a Huey after heavy contact with the VC in the *Suoi Da* area during OPERATION GOLDEN GATE. (US Army)

Project Leaping Lena/Project Delta

In May of 1964 PROJECT LEAPING LENA was initiated. Under this project's auspices US Special Forces began training LLDB and CIDG personnel in long-range reconnaissance techniques. After the transfer of Special Forces Operations to MACV under OPERATION SWITCHBACK LEAPING LENA would become PROJECT DELTA, the first of various special projects carried out by Special Forces and indigenous troops. During its early stages only one A-Detachment was assigned to DELTA, although the commitment would grow until almost 100 US Special Forces personnel were assigned. As the importance of DELTA's covert reconnaissance mission grew, Detachment B-52 was activated in June of 1965, to control it. Under B-52 DELTA was organized into twelve reconnaissance teams (later expanded to sixteen teams) consisting of two US Special Forces and four *indigs* each. (Actually, each team consisted of four US Special Forces and six *indigs*, but on operations only six were normally deployed.) Six (later expanded to twelve) CIDG 'Roadrunner' teams of four *indigs* each, operated along VC/NVA trail networks dressed as VC; a *Nung* camp security company (also used for other special duties such as bomb damage assessment missions); and a Vietnamese Ranger battalion was used as a reaction force. The 281st Assault Helicopter Company was assigned to provide air support. These reconnaissance and 'Roadrunner' teams would carry out intelligence, hunter-killer raids, deception missions, etc, calling in the reaction forces if necessary to deal with enemy troops encountered. Early infiltrations were usually carried out by night parachute drop, but helicopter insertions and other methods were used later. DELTA was based at *Nha Trang* with many other important Special Forces activities.

PROJECT DELTA would remain active until June of 1970, and would eventually reach a strength of over 1,200 indigenous personnel assigned. In addition to carrying out their own reconnaissance missions, in September of 1966 DELTA was given responsibility for training US infantry as well as *indigs* in long range patrolling at the 5th Special Forces Group (Abn) Reconnaissance School.

Members of III Corps MIKE Force under attack by the VC during OPERATION GOLDEN GATE in November of 1966. They carry M1 Carbines which were standard for MIKE Forces and CIDG units until MIKE Forces received priority issuance of M-16s after the Tet Offensive. (US Army)

Members of III Corps MIKE Force returning from a search and destroy mission during OPERATION GOLDEN GATE in November of 1966. Most members of this unit wear tiger stripes and carry M1 Carbines. Although this MIKE Force was a *nung* unit, the man in the mid-foreground wearing the green utilities and carrying a BAR appears to be a Montagnard or perhaps a Cambodian. (US Army photo)

Members of CIDG Company 354 along with their advisors from Special Forces Detachment A-321 hit Landing Zone *Tien Thuan* at the beginning of OPERATION RENEGADE in November of 1966. (US Army)

(Above) A C-123 drops supplies to Special Forces Detachment A-101 at Khe Sanh in January of 1967. (US Army)

XM177E2 Submachine Gun

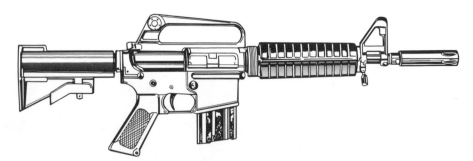

(Right) During March of 1967 a sergeant of Detachment A-301 gives instruction in the use of the M-79 grenade launcher at the Trung Sap III Corps CIDG training center. The well faded tiger striped 'boonie hat' worn by this Special Forces instructor was very popular among special ops troops as well as the *indigs* they trained. (US Army)

(Left) 32S-3 transmitter used at the Nha Trang 'Mars' Station to maintain communications with A-Detachments. (US Army)

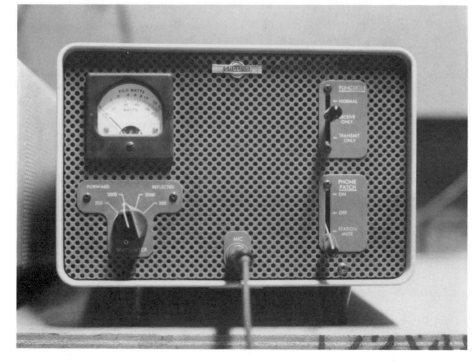

(Above) Antenna of the Mars Station at Nha Trang as it appeared during late September of 1967. This radio station was used for communication with Special Forces units throughout Vietnam. (US Army)

(Left) The radio control box of the Mars Station communications system at Nha Trang. (US Army)

Formation of the MIKE Forces

As the CIDG program became more successful VC and NVA regulars began giving them more and more attention, mounting heavier and heavier attacks on their camps. In response to this, in October of 1964 the foundations were laid for the Mobile Strike Forces (MIKE Forces) which would come into existence in mid-1965. A Mobile Strike Force initially consisted of three companies and an HQ having a total strength of about 600 men, and was an elite element within the CIDG which could react quickly to enemy attacks on CIDG camps. Trained as airborne/airmobile troops, MIKE Force companies were not only used as a reaction element, but could carry out offensive raids, combat patrols, or ambushes. Since MIKE Forces came directly under US Special Forces control and were commanded by members of the US Special Forces rather than the LLDB, MIKE Forces could be used more aggressively and independently. Because of their combat ability and loyalty to the Americans, *Nung* tribesman were heavily represented in the early MIKE Forces. During June of 1965 a MIKE Force battalion was authorized for each C-Detachment, and one was assigned to Nha Trang directly under 5th SFG (Abn) control. In December of 1966 MIKE Forces came under joint US/Vietnamese Special Forces control, but until that time they had taken orders strictly from US Special Forces. Even after that date, for all practical purposes, US Special Forces retained operational control of MIKE Forces. The controlling Special Forces detachment for Mobile Strike Force Command was Detachment B-55.

(Below) During September of 1967 a UH-1C Huey 'slick' (transport) chopper lands on a mountain top landing zone to resupply members of the 5th SFG(Abn) and the 125th Signal Company who manned an important radio relay site. (US Army)

(Above) CIDG members at a camp in the Mekong Delta man a .50 caliber machine gun mounted on the top of the inner flood dikes built to protect the camp during the rainy season. This unit was advised by Detachment A-433. The Colored scarves are worn as a unit distinction. (US Army)

(Below) Members of a CIDG unit located near My An are manning an airboat which is used to patrol the 'Plain of Reeds' and interdict VC supply lines in July of 1967. This CIDG unit was advised by Detachment A-433. (US Army)

14

(Above) An Airboat patrol unit of the IV Corps MIKE Force prior to setting out on a patrol in the Mekong Delta during August of 1967. The tiger stripe camouflage utilities predominate, while the spotted pattern, often associated with the National Police Field Force and the PRUs, is seen only on the shirt of the man in the right foreground, who wears his MIKE Force insignia as a beret badge. The weapons mounted on the bow of the boats are Browning Model 1919 machine guns. (US Army)

(Above Right) A Special Forces instructor of Detachment A-503 instructs a Mobile Strike Forces trooper in proper parachute techniques at Nha Trang during October of 1967. This sergeant still wears the early 5th SFG(Abn) beret flash rather than the later flash which incorporated the colors of the Vietnamese flag. Note also the MIKE Force pocket patch and tape above the pocket and parachutist's and combat infantry badges worn on the breast of his tiger stripe camouflage utilities. (US Army)

Swedish K Submachine Gun
Sound-Suppressed

(Right) During December of 1967 a Special Forces advisor at Nha Trang supervises MIKE Forces troops in hand-to-hand combat training. (US Army)

Special Forces advisor test fires an M79 grenade launcher. (Larry Dring photo)

Special Forces advisor in tiger stripes and 'boonie hat' on patrol with CIDG troops. (Larry Dring photo)

(Above) Special Forces advisors on patrol with the CIDG unit they advise wearing typical field attire and equipment. An M18 smoke grenade is carried on the webbed gear of the man on the left. A Montagnard bracelet is worn on the wrist of the trooper at the right. (Larry Dring photo)

This Special Forces advisor on patrol with his CIDG unit wears a 'boonie hat' and locally made tiger stripes. A .45 caliber automatic is worn in a shoulder holster. (Larry Dring photo)

Special Forces advisor waits for an extraction chopper amidst purple marking smoke from an M18 grenade. The logs in the foreground are the remains of trees felled when the landing zone was cleared. (Larry Dring photo)

(Right) Special Forces CIDG camp at *Thien Ngon* viewed from the air shows the arrangement of the five pointed star outer defensive perimeter and a circular trench surrounding a five sided inner defense.

Special Forces Beret Badge

(Right) This Special Forces fighting camp viewed from the air shows the inner and outer defense works pock marked with mortar pits. US Special Forces and LLDB usually would occupy the inner defensive positions, often with a *Nung* detachment. The arsenal and communications center would normally be located in the center. The outer perimeter was usually manned by CIDG troops.

(Above) Special Forces camp at *Bu Nard* advised by Detachment A-344 has defenses that included mortars that are backed up by 105mm howitzers.

(Left) This smaller Special Forces camp located with its back to a river illustrates how camps were usually constructed to take advantage of local terrain and the size of the defending forces.

(Below) The Special Forces camp located at *Ton Le Chon* has less sophisticated defenses than many camps but still has both inner and outer defensive perimeters.

CIDG Program at its Peak

The shift towards more offensive operations on the part of CIDG units coincided with the buildup of conventional US forces in Vietnam during 1965 and 1966. As a result, CIDG and other Special Forces trained indigenous troops often acted as scouts for US ground units and stalking horses for US airmobile units such as the 1st Air Cavalry or the 173rd Airborne Brigade which would be called in when the *cidgees* drew fire. Unfortunately, conventional US commanders frequently did not understand that the CIDG units were *irregulars* and had to be employed as such to be effective. The greatest contribution of the CIDG units — including DELTA and the later 'Greeks' (SIGMA, OMEGA, and GAMMA) — was in the area of intelligence gathering. As the value of their intelligence gathering was realized by MACV both the 5th SFG (Abn) and their indigenous strength continued to increase in order to fulfill the additional missions assigned to them, and by July of 1966 the 5th Special Forces Group (Airborne) strength stood at 2,627, and the camp strike force strength was at 33,400 backed up by 2,400 MIKE Forces. By October of 1966 there were ninety-seven Special Forces camps in Vietnam.

As PROJECTS SIGMA and OMEGA — special reconnaissance projects similar to PROJECT DELTA — got underway in 1966, MIKE Forces began to see increasing offensive action in response to intelligence gathered by DELTA, SIGMA and OMEGA. Among these operations were BLACKJACK 33 and BLACKJACK 41, the former of which was highly successful, inflicting some 300 VC casualties, due to the efforts of a mobile guerrilla force commanded by 'Bo' Gritz. BLACKJACK 41 involved a parachute assault by 373 members of the MIKE Forces and twenty-one members of US Special Forces on 13 May 1967.

BLACKJACK operations normally were the result of a MIKE Force recon platoon or a Mobile Guerrilla Force (consisting of a MIKE Force company and a recon platoon) being inserted and then reinforced by battalions of the MIKE Force to act upon the intelligence gathered or contact made by the recon troops. BLACKJACK OPS also included ambushing VC couriers or paymasters, destroying or boobytrapping weapons or food caches, and doing whatever possible to harass the enemy in his *safe* areas. Members of the recon platoons were often graduates of the reconnaissance school established at Nha Trang by members of PROJECT DELTA to train their own personnel. US Long Range Reconnaissance Patrols (LRRPs, pronounced *lirps*) were also trained at the MACV Reconnaissance/Commando (Recondo) School established in September of 1966, as an offshoot of the 5th SFG (Abn) Reconnaissance School, as were reconnaissance troops from Vietnam, Korea, and other allied countries. The three week recondo course included helicopter insertions and extractions, escape and evasion, survival, familiarity with the PRC-25, HT-1, and URC-10 radios, intelligence gathering including photography, long range patrolling, enemy weapons, and *other special subjects*. Normally, each class consisted of sixty students. Members of DELTA, SIGMA, and OMEGA teams were also trained at the facility, though not necessarily as part of the normal Recondo classes. Parachute training was also offered to those not already airborne qualified and in need of such training.

As of July, 1968, MIKE Force strength was divided as follows:

5th Mobile Strike Force Command assigned directly under the control of 5th SFG(Abn) — approximately 2,500 men in four battalions, one reconnaissance company, and an HQ.
1st Mobile Strike Force Command assigned to I Corps and controlled by Detachment B-16-1 — 463 men in two battalions, one reconnaissance company, and an HHQ.
2nd Mobile Strike Force Command assigned to II Corps and controlled by B-20 — 3,119 men in five battalions, one reconnaissance company, and an HHC.
3rd Mobile Strike Force Command assigned to III Corps and controlled by B-36 — 2,015 men consisting of three battalions, one reconnaissance company, and an HHC.
4th Mobile Strike Force Command assigned to IV Corps and controlled by B-40 — 2,199 men consisting of three battalions, one airboat company, one reconnaissance company, and an HHC. The airboat company assigned to 4th MSFC was necessary for operating in the Mekong Delta, especially during the rainy season.

Special Forces advisor from Detachment A-411 patrols the river from the CIDG camp at *My Phuc Tay* in IV Corps during the summer of 1968. He wears a 'duck hunter' camo shirt and tiger striped trousers. (US Army)

1st MSFC was based at Da Nang, **2nd MSFC** at Plieku, **3rd MSFC** at Long Hai, and **4th MSFC** at Can Tho. **5th MSFC** was normally based at Nha Trang but was used all over the country as the group commander needed them. By 1966 and continuing through the late 1960s, MIKE Forces were used in some of the most hotly contested areas in Vietnam such as War Zones C and D.

Throughout the 1960s, Special Forces continued to be involved in civic action and Psychological Operations (Psy Ops), but the primary emphasis was now on intelligence gathering and offensive operations. Combining both civic action and military advisory missions, Special Forces A-Detachment COs often advised local district officials and helped train the Regional and Popular Forces (Ruff Puffs) which came under the local official's command.

PROJECT DELTA continued to grow in importance as did other intelligence missions. By 1967 DELTA had expanded to sixteen recon teams, each composed of four *indigs* and two US Special Forces (though under Major Allen, the DELTA commander between 1967 and 1968 there were normally three US personnel on each recon team during operations), eight Roadrunner teams, and a reaction force of six ARVN Ranger companies. DELTA operations continued to stress the insertion of teams into VC controlled territory primarily to gather intelligence but occasionally to attack targets of opportunity. Other special operations had been carried out since January of 1964 by MACV/SOG, which will be discussed separately from the CIDG Program.

Another interesting Special Forces trained special operations unit which came into existence during the mid-1960s was 'Apache Force' which was made up of indigenous CIDG troops and Special Forces advisors who specialized in orienting US ground troops for operations in Vietnam. After orientation sessions, the Apache Force would normally accompany conventional troops on operations for their first few days on the line. The Apache Force evolved into Combat Recon Patrols which proved so effective during BLACKJACK OPERATIONS and In other aspects of the aggressive use of CIDG units.

By 1967, new CIDG camps being constructed were 'fighting camps' designed to withstand heavy enemy attack with pre-planned defenses in depth. CIDG night operations began to be stressed with a resulting jump in the number of enemy killed. No longer did the VC own the night. By 1967, PROJECT OMEGA and SIGMA had joined DELTA in full operation and were bringing in valuable intelligence. Though not a hard-and-fast rule, DELTA operated mainly in I Corps, OMEGA in II Corps, and SIGMA in III Corps. Because of close cooperation between US Special Forces and the Vietnamese Special Forces (LLDB), the LLDB began to show marked improvement during 1966 and 1967. Much of the credit for this improvement goes to US Special Forces Detachment B-51 assigned to the LLDB training center at Dong Ba Thin. Other B-Detachments in-country during 1967 included B-50 assigned to PROJECT OMEGA, B-52 assigned to PROJECT DELTA, B-53 assigned to ARVN airborne ranger training center, B-55 assigned to the 5th Mobile Strike Force Command, B-56 assigned to PROJECT SIGMA, and B-57 assigned to PROJECT GAMMA. It should be noted that PROJECT GAMMA was implemented in June of 1967, to gather intelligence about NVA bases and infiltration routes in Cambodia. Improvement in the LLDB was such that in 1967 it became practical to once again turn a number of CIDG camps over to them.

The Special Forces' plan for use of the CIDG during 1967 and 1968 foresaw the emphasis remaining on CIDG border surveillance camps and camps positioned to interdict the infiltration routes. Most camps built during this time period were assigned one or both of these primary missions. In the Mekong Delta, Special Forces fighting camps were often designed to be floating camps which could remain in operation even when the Delta were flooded. Aggressive patrolling by CIDG units in the Delta contributed greatly toward clearing the VC from the Plain of Reeds.

Early in 1967 Special Forces-advised CIDG units began operating from camps opened in war Zone C, which had been a notorious VC stronghold for years. Other heavily contested areas also came under CIDG control during this period as camps were opened where they would do the most good in the overall strategic plan for conduct of the war. Some of these new camps came under heavy attack by VC and NVA regulars. Two which withstood particularly heavy attacks during May of 1967, were Lang Vei and Con Thien. The availability of the MIKE Forces for rapid reinforcement combined with the availability of American airpower played a key role in preventing the fall of some camps. As previously mentioned, MIKE Forces were also used extensively for offensive operations unrelated to the defense of the CIDG camps. All MIKE Forces units, but especially the *Nung* ones, proved so effective, in fact, that between June of 1966, and June of 1967, Mobile Strike Force strength was doubled. MIKE Force companies had a normal strength of 185 men organized into three rifle platoons, a weapons platoon, and a small HQ. Though lightly armed for conducting operations in the rear of the enemy, MIKE Forces could call in artillery or air support as needed, depending on their location or mission. Normally, mortars, M60 GPMGs, and M79 grenade launchers were the heaviest weapons in the weapons platoon's TOE, though in certain situations, LAWs or other weapons might be issued.

To short circuit the corruption in the Vietnamese logistics system, the CIDG program and other Special Forces operations had their own logistics system based on forward supply points in each of the four corps tactical zones. Resupply for fighting camps was rapid, often using aerial resupply. The US Army Counterinsurgency Support Office, which had been established on Okinawa on 27 February 1963, took care of acquiring locally any special equipment or supplies needed by the Special Forces or their indigenous troops. Everything from rucksacks to special rations which were the forerunners of LRRP rations for CIDG and SOG recon teams to 'sterile' weapons passed through their supply channels.

A heavy weapons leader from Detachment A-244 looks on as a CIDG 105ᴍᴍ howitzer crew prepares to load and fire their weapon at *Ben Het* in November of 1969. (US Army)

In January of 1970 a group of Montangards prepare to move out of the Bu Prang Special Forces camp on a patrol. In November of 1970, this CIDG unit was converted to ARVN Ranger status. (US Army)

Two Special Forces advisors from Detachment A-242 instruct a CIDG trooper from the camp at Dak Pek on how to set a demolition charge in February of 1970. (US Army)

Special Forces camp at Dak Pek after being hit hard by an enemy attack during February of 1970. (US Army)

The Chopper pad of the 7th Aviation Company which served Special Forces. Detachment A-242 at Dak Pek under rocket attack from North Vietnamese regulars during February of 1970. (US Army)

A Special Forces medical supervisor of Detachment A-242 cleans the wound of a villager after an NVA attack in November of 1970. This medic wears parachutist's wings on his left breast. All Special Forces were fully airborne qualified. (US Army)

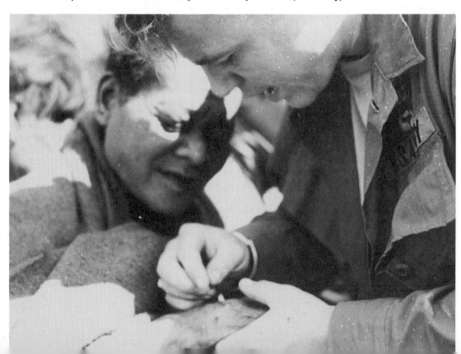

Tet Offensive

CIDG units, especially MIKE Forces and the Greek letter units, had proven their value at intelligence gathering and at wresting control of contested areas from the VC, and when the Tet Offensive hit the populated areas of South Vietnam on 29 January 1968 the *cidgees* proved themselves to be tenacious fighters in built-up areas as well. Fortunately for the government of South Vietnam some VC detachments launched their attacks prematurely against cities such as Ban Me Thuot and Nha Trang garrisoned by MIKE Forces which bloodied Charley's nose early in the Tet Offensive. Such important centers of Special Forces activity as Ban Me Thuot, Nha Trang, and Kontum were well-defended by members of Special Forces, *Nung* security detachments, and MIKE Force troops. OMEGA personnel also aided in the defense of Ban Me Thuot, and DELTA and GAMMA personnel were involved in defending Nha Trang.

Cidgees also contributed heavily to the defense of Qui Nhon, Pleiku, Chau Doc, Phan Thiet, and Dalat. Pleiku was the base for Detachment C-2 and the 2nd Mobile Strike Force Command, while Chau Doc was the base for Detachment B-42 with its attached irregulars. Each of the other cities had Special Forces and irregulars based in their environs or nearby.

During the build-up for the Tet Offensive and during it, most of the CIDG camps other than those in I Corps were left alone as VC strength was concentrated around Khe Sanh. However some Special Forces camps came under attack, particularly Lang Vei under Detachment A-101. Lang Vei's history had been an active one, since its establishment in December of 1966. On 4 May 1967, the camp had been virtually destroyed in an attack aided by VC who had infiltrated the CIDG units in the camp. Finally, on 7 February 1968 the camp was overrun by enemy forces which included NVA tanks.

As the VC remnants, who had survived the assaults on the cities, retreated after Tet, CIDG units punished them severely by striking them along their infiltration/exfiltration routes.

The excellent performance of the *cidgees* during Tet caused certain changes in the way they were viewed by MACV and the South Vietnamese military hierarchy. CIDG units were given greater responsibility in defending II, III, and IV Corps as conventional ARVN units were moved into I Corps to resecure areas occupied by the VC and NVA during the Tet Offensive. As a result of their good showing, in April of 1968 CIDG units were given priority in weapons modernization as they received M-16 assault rifles, M-60 GPMGs, and M-79 grenade launchers.

MIKE Force strength was also greatly increased. By the summer of 1968, there were thirty-four MIKE Force companies — five in I Corps (Da Nang), twelve in II Corps (*Pleiku, Ban Me Thuot, Kontum,* and *Qui Nhon*), seven in III Corps (*Lang Hai*), and ten in IV Corps (*Dan Phuc, Moc Hoa, To Chau,* an *Cao Lanh*). By the fall of 1968, 5th Special Forces Group strength was over 3,500 with over 27,000 CIDG and over 7,000 MIKE Force personnel under their supervision.

Vietnamization

Beginning early in 1968 the process of turning over CIDG camps to Vietnamese control was speeded up. MACV also developed the concept of using CIDG personnel primarily along the western borders of Vietnam to interdict infiltration routes. More and more responsibility, from C-Detachment down through A-Detachment level, was turned over to the LLDB to prepare them for the eventual complete turn-over of the CIDG program. Emphasis was also placed on turning over civic action and Psy Ops to the Vietnamese.

During 1969 as the LLDB became more competent, turnover of the strategically important border surveillance and interdiction camps to South Vietnamese control began. Nevertheless, US Special Forces strength in Vietnam peaked during 1969, with over 4,000

(Above) At Dak Pek during June of 1970 Special Forces ordnance experts of Detachment A29 prepare to burn small arms ammunition with diesel fuel. (US Army)

Special Forces troopers assigned (including those on special operations such as SOG). By early 1970, in fact, it had been decided to end the CIDG program and to absorb CIDG units into the Army of the Republic of Vietnam. As a result during the fall of 1970 a few camps were closed down, and thirty-seven were converted to ARVN Ranger camps with their CIDG complement becoming ARVN Ranger battalions, primarily 'Border Rangers'. As Special Forces responsibilities were terminated the 5th Special Forces Group (Airborne) strength began to decline, dropping to under 3,000 by late 1970.

During 1970 CIDG units along with members of US Special Forces participated in operations in Cambodia between 29 April and 30 June 1970. CIDG companies from *Duc Hue* and *Tra Cu* played an especially important role in Cambodia as they assaulted a VC training area and discovered large caches of crew served weapons and other equipment.

On 31 December 1970, participation of the 5th SFG (Abn) in the CIDG Program officially terminated. On 3 March 1971 the 5th SFG(Abn) officially departed Vietnam for Fort Bragg, although some Special Forces troopers assigned to advisory missions or special operations would remain much longer. During the 1972 Communist Easter Offensive, a limited number of Special Forces personnel who had previously served in Vietnam returned for temporary duty. As in the early days of Special Forces involvement in Vietnam, Special Forces personnel were reportedly assigned to the CIA and operating in-country during the final days before the fall of South Vietnam.

Special Forces instructor of Detachment B-51 at the basic airborne school at *Dong Ba Thin* briefs trainees prior to the mock door phase of their training. May 1970. (US Army)

(Left) Two members of USAF's Combat Control Team (CCT) direct an incoming transport aircraft at the landing strip of a Special Forces camp during August of 1968.

(Right) During early 1963 a US Army Ranger advisor to the ARVN Rangers uses his Randall Attack/Survival Knife to cut the ignition cord for an M18A1 Claymore mine while instructing the kneeling BDQ in the use of this device.

(Above) US LRRP of Company N, 75th Infantry (Ranger), 173rd Airborne Brigade checks a shotgun shell before loading it into his Ithaca shotgun prior to a mission during March of 1971. His captured Tokarev M-51 pistol is worn in a makeshift holster originally intended for a S&W .38 caliber Special revolver.

(Above Right) LRRP of Company F, 58th Infantry (Long Range Patrol), 101st Airborne Division on patrol during June of 1968 in *Thua Thien* Province as part of OPERATION NEVADA EAGLE. The pocket patch worn on the left pocket identifies him as a graduate of the MACV Recondo School at *Nha Trang*. His M-16 rifle mounts an AN/PVS-2 starlight scope, possibly indicating his assignment to a night ambush team.

(Right) Two Special Forces recon troopers assigned to 'PROJECT DELTA' are being extracted via STABO rig during an operation late in 1969.

(Above) Son Tay Raider on 21 November 1970 prepares to move through a doorway in the prison compound. His XM177E2 has an Aimpoint sight taped to the carry handle. These sights were acquired from private sources since there was not a satisfactory lightweight sight of this type in the Army logistics system.

(Above) A US Special Forces NCO assigned to a MACV/SOG Recon Team in Command Control Central (CCC) is alert to the possible presence of the enemy while on a reconnaissance mission into Cambodia during April of 1970, prior to the 'incursion' into that country. His weapon is a suppressed Swedish 'K' SMG, and he wears a STABO rig for helicopter extraction.

(Right) During November of 1964, a Special Forces captain instructs a Montagnard Strike Force member in the procedure for loading the M3A1 'Grease Gun'. The Special Forces officer wears a Randall fighting knife on his hip, and a Rolex watch, one of the most prized possessions in Vietnam, on his wrist.

MACV/SOG

Separate from 'conventional', *unconventional operations* of the 5th Special Forces Group were the clandestine operations of Military Assistance Command Vietnam/Studies and Observations Group (MACV/SOG). The Studies and Observations Group (SOG) was a cover name to disguise SOG's real function, and the name 'Special Operations Group', as it was sometimes called, described its real mission more accurately.

Activated in January of 1964, SOG was a joint services unit composed of members from all four branches of the armed forces, including Navy SEALS, Marine Recons, Air Force special operations pilots of the 90th Special Operations Wing, but predominantly Army Special Forces. Naval craft were made available for clandestine insertions into North Vietnam. Assigned to MACV/SOG, Navy SEALS reportedly became most familiar with Haiphong Harbor. Working closely with the CIA, SOG carried out clandestine operations all over Southeast Asia, and although supervised by MACV, SOG came directly under control of the Joint Chiefs of Staff through the Special Assistant for Counterinsurgency and Special Activities. Among other duties, SOG worked closely with the Vietnamese Special Exploitation Service (SES), which became the Strategic Technical Directorate in September of 1967, to carry out sabotage, Psy Ops, intelligence, and other *special missions*. Among the many excellent officers assigned to SOG were Colonel Donald Blackburn (who in World War II had led a Philippine guerrilla unit known as 'Blackburn's Headhunters') and Colonel John Singlaub, both commanders of MACV/SOG, and Colonel 'Bull' Simons who commanded CPS 35 under Blackburn and organized many of the covert missions into Laos (where he had earlier worked as CO of WHITE STAR), Cambodia, and North Vietnam.

At its peak, MACV/SOG had some 2,000 Americans and over 8,000 *indigs* assigned. A larger percentage of the Americans were Special Forces personnel whose assignment to SOG was covered by assignment to a 5th SFG (Abn) unit euphemistically known as Special Operations Augmentation. Many members of the 1st SFG (Abn) on Okinawa volunteered for TDY tours with SOG as did a substantial number of men from the 7th SFG(Abn).

MACV/SOG's missions included: cross border operations into Cambodia, Laos, and North Vietnam to carry out intelligence gathering or raiding missions on the enemy's 'home ground'; gathering intelligence about POWs and carrying out rescue missions when possible; rescuing downed aircrews in enemy territory ('Bright Light' missions); training, inserting, and controlling agents in North Vietnam to gather intelligence or form resistance groups; carrying out 'black' Psy Ops such as operating fake broadcasting stations inside North Vietnam; kidnapping or assassinating key enemy personnel; retrieving sensitive documents or equipment lost in enemy territory or in enemy hands; and inserting rigged mortar rounds or other booby-trapped ordnance in enemy arms caches (OPERATION ELDEST SON).

Among SOG special missions were those carried out under the code name OPERATION SHINING BRASS against NVA infiltration routes in Laos. Carried out by twelve man teams (three Americans and nine *Yards* or *Nungs*), SHINING BRASS missions were primarily intended to locate targets for bombing or for gunship ('Spooky,' 'Spectre,' etc) attacks, but sometimes reaction forces were called in after contact was made by the recon team.

SHINING BRASS missions were normally limited to areas near the Vietnamese/Laotian border, but later other special missions into Laos were carried out by Mobile Launch Team-3 from Nakhon Phanom, Thailand. Similar cross border reconnaissance operations were carried out into Cambodia. Between 1965 and 1972, a total of 2,675 cross border operations were carried out with a total of 103 US Special Forces casualties on such missions. *Indig* casualties were much higher. The relatively low number of US casualties should not be considered an indication of lack of danger, however; these missions were highly dangerous, but the US troops assigned to SOG were of such high caliber that they took lighter casualties than troops with lesser training would have taken. Nevertheless, some reconnaissance teams were never heard from again, seeming to have disappeared

General Abrams meets with US and Vietnamese personnel at MACV/SOG Command Control North (CCN) at DaNang during 1970. The beret badge of the ARVN officer at the left indicates that he is assigned to an airborne unit rather than an LLDB unit. (Larry Greene and Society of Vietnamese Rangers)

from the face of the earth, and others took very heavy casualties.

SOG's headquarters was located in Saigon near Tan Son Nhut Air Base. But while missions were normally planned at SOG HQ, missions were normally implemented or 'launched' from forward sites known as Forward Operations Bases (FOBs), later called Command and Control sites. Somtimes special missions were launched by 'Mobile Launch Teams', such as the one mentioned earlier at Nakhon Phanom. FOB-1 was located at Ban Me Thuot, FOB-2 at Kontum, FOB-3 at Khe Sanh, and FOB-4 at Da Nang.

Three 'Command and Control' units were formed in November of 1967, succeeding and consolidating the four FOBs.

Command and Control North (CCN) based at *Da Nang*, coordinated missions into Laos and North Vietnam (including 'Kit-Cat' missions deep in North Vietnam). Laos missions fell under OPERATION SHINING BRASS and PRAIRIE FIRE, while missions into North Vietnam were usually under OPERATION PLAN 34A. CCN was the largest of the Command and Control, with 'launch' sites at *Hue-Phu Bai, Khe Sanh, Quan Tri*, and *Kham Duc.*

Command and Control Central based at *Kontum*, carried out missions in the area where the borders of South Vietnam, Cambodia, and Laos meet.

Command and Control South (CCS) at *Ban Me Thout* was the smallest of the three Command and Control units and controlled missions into Cambodia.

CCN, CCC, and CCS were organized along similar lines. Their primary operational element was the Spike Reconnaissance Team, each consisting of three US Special Forces and nine indigenous personnel. These Reconnaissance Teams (RTs) were named primarily after states or snakes, although the RTs assigned to CCS tended to be named after implements or things relating to the weather. The total number of RTs available at SOG's peak was around seventy. Hatchet Forces backed up the RTs. Consisting of five US Special Forces and thirty *indigs*, Hatchet Forces were assigned missions requiring more men than were available in an RT. Hatchet Forces, for example, specialized in ambushing NVA or VC troops infiltrating into South Vietnam. Search-Locate-Annihilate-Mission (SLAM) companies acted as a reaction force for the RTs or were inserted to exploit RT information or situations. The three Command and Control units were shut down in March of 1971, being replaced by Task Force 1 Advisory Element at Da Nang until MACV/SOG was deactivated in April of 1972. Despite this deactivation, during April of 1972 many former SOG troopers were rushed back to Vietnam to help call in air strikes or carry out special missions in I Corps Tactical Zone during the Easter Invasion of South Vietnam. Certain special operations continued under the Technical Directorate Assistance Team 158, which was activated on 1 May 1972 as the successor to SOG. This unit operated until 12 March 1973 when it was deactivated. Officially this ended US special operations in Vietnam, but reportedly, certain US special operations personnel remained active in South Vietnam until after the fall of Saigon, and substantially beyond!

RECONNAISSANCE TEAMS KNOWN TO HAVE BEEN ASSIGNED TO A SPECIFIC COMMAND AND CONTROL

CCN	CCC	CCS
RT Adder	RT Alabama	RT Fork
RT Alaska	RT Arizona	RT Lightning
RT Anaconda	RT Arkansas	RT Mike Facs
RT Asp	RT California	RT Plane
RT Bushmaster	RT Colorado	RT Spike
RT Connecticut	RT Delaware	RT Trowel
RT Crusader	RT Hotcake	RT Weather
RT Hawaii	RT Illinois	
RT Hunter	RT Iowa	
RT Idaho	RT Kentucky	
RT Indiana	RT Montana	
RT Intruder	RT Nevada	
RT Kansas	RT New Mexico	
RT Krait	RT Texas	
RT Louisiana	RT Vermont	
RT Mamba	RT Washington	
RT Mississippi	RT West Virginia	
RT Missouri		
RT Moccasin		
RT New Jersey		
RT North Carolina		
RT Ohio		
RT Rhode Island		
RT Rattler		
RT Sidewinder		
RT Viper		
RT Virginia		
RT Wasp		

(Above) MACV/SOG Reconnaissance Team prior to a mission out of MLT-1 at Phu Bai during 1970. Team members are armed with CAR-15s and wear the Maguire (also known as STABO) rig for helicopter extraction while leaving the arms free to operate weapons if necessary. The use of Olive Drab towels or scarves as headgear was common among SOG personnel. Other than the American at right the members of this team are obviously *Nung* Chinese. (Don Valentie/Society of Vietnamese Rangers)

RANDALL Model 14 Attack Knife

Heavy brass guard with a 7 1/2 inch blade and a plastic Micarta handle.

(Right) US advisors to the Quang Tin Province PRUs along with a field expedient coastal patrol craft assembled by the advisors. Tiger stripes (with the exception of the man on the right) and Green berets are worn.

28

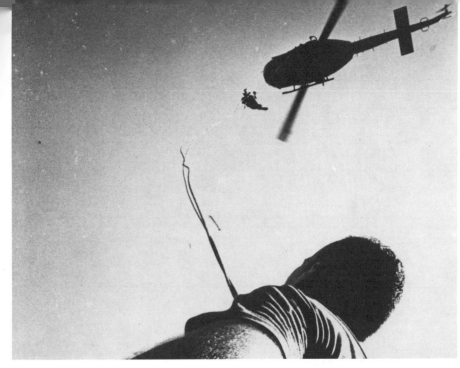

During the fall of 1968 an instructor at the MACV Recondo School acts as an anchor man while a student makes his first descent from a UH-1D Huey helicopter. (US Army)

A MACV Recondo School instructor discusses the drop with a student who has just descended from the 40 foot tower during a fall of 1968 course. Gloves and the ubiquitous 'boonie hat' are worn by the student, who is most likely a LRRP from one of the divisions or brigades. (US Army)

A student at the MACV Recondo School at Nha Trang begins his descent from a UH-1D Huey during his training in the fall of 1968. This student is wearing tiger stripes and carries full equipment. The use of full equipment was typical of the Recondo School which stressed realistic training including field exercises which often resulted in VC contacts. (US Army)

The Son Tay Raid

In May of 1970, Special Assistant for Counterinsurgency and Special Activities (SACSA) Brigadier General Donald Blackburn got the go-ahead from the Joint Chiefs of Staff (JCS) to begin planning a rescue mission into North Vietnam to free POWs believed to be held at Son Tay Prison located twenty-three miles from Hanoi. By 5 June 1970, a briefing had been given the Joint Chiefs about a possible rescue mission. Within a few days, Blackburn was given the go-ahead to continue planning the raid, and on 10 July Blackburn received the OK from the Joint Chiefs to implement his recommendation.

Originally, General Blackburn had wanted to lead the raid himself, however, his knowledge of sensitive intelligence matters automatically precluded him. Instead, the assignment went to Colonel 'Bull' Simons, a highly experienced Special Forces officer who had served under Blackburn with MACV/SOG. The raiding party commanded by Simons was code named 'Joint Contingency Task Group' (JCTG), and the mission was code named 'Ivory Coast'. For training JCTG personnel an area of Eglin Air Force Base was set aside. Air Force Brigadier General Leroy Manor, CO of Air Force special operations assets at Eglin AFB, was put in overall command, while his deputy, Col 'Bull' Simons, would lead the actual raid.

Since the optimum time for the raid appeared to be between 20 and 25 October, both men immediately began selecting their teams — Manor the air and planning elements and Simons the raiding force. At Fort Bragg, hundreds of Special Forces soldiers volunteered for the JCTG knowing only that it was 'hazardous' and the 'Bull' would be commanding. Fifteen officers and eighty-two NCOs, primarily from the 6th and 7th SFGs, were selected, from which the assault force, their backups, and support personnel would be chosen. A mock-up of the Son Tay Compound was built at Eglin for training. So Soviet spy satellites could not reveal its presence, the mock-up was designed to be dismantled during the day and quickly set up at night for training. Since the raid itself would be at night, training on the mock-up was at night. A $60,000 table top model of the camp was also built which included the capability of viewing the model under different types of lighting to duplicate moonlight, flares, etc.

Training of the raiding force began on 9 September 1970. Intensive training was given in night firing, hand signals, immediate action drills, house clearing, radio procedures, emergency medical techniques, and other skills already possessed to a greater or lesser degree by the raiders, who were highly trained Special Forces troops. The assault force was formed into three groups — the compound assault force of fourteen men who would actually land inside the prison compound; the command and security staff of twenty men; and the support group of twenty-two men. Simons himself commanded the support group. Beginning on 28 September the assault force practiced the actual assault with the Air Force crews who would fly the helicopters and other aircraft. The landing and assault were rehearsed again and again with many being 'live fire' run throughs. Alternative plans were also practiced in case one of the three teams failed to make it to the target.

On 27 October, Blackburn got the go ahead to begin moving personnel to Southeast Asia in preparation for the mission. On 1 November 1970 Blackburn and Simons, among others, left for Southeast Asia to lay the groundwork for the raid. By 12 November, both Blackburn and Simons were back in the States as the raiding force prepared to head for Thailand. On 18 November the President gave the 'GO' order for the raid; the raiders had left for Takhli RTAFB, Thailand a few hours previously in anticipation of receiving permission to carry out the raid. The weather had to be right for the operation to have a reasonable chance of success, and there had to be a one-quarter to three-quarter moon so the raiders would have acceptable light on the ground. Conditions were deemed acceptable to launch the raid on the night of 20/21 November.

On the evening of 20 November the raiders were shuttled to Udorn RTAFB from where the raid would be launched at 2318 local time. To create a diversion while the raid was underway, carrier based naval aircraft would be sent over Hanoi during the early hours of 21 November.

A student from Company L (Ranger), 75th Infantry, 101st Airborne Division ties a Claymore mine on a tree to clear a landing site on Hon Tri Island during a training exercise at the MACV Recondo School. (US Army)

At about 0218, Hanoi time, 21 November, the raid itself began. As a C-130 Hercules flare ship illuminated the area with flares, an HH-53, codenamed 'Apple Three,' opened up on the guard towers on Son Tay Prison with twin Gatling guns, bringing them crashing down.

Shortly thereafter, the HH-3 carrying the assault party landed inside the prison compound. A few minutes later the command and security group landed just outside the prison's walls. The support group led by Simons himself, however, had landed some 400 meters off course at what was labeled on the raiders' maps as a 'secondary school'. Instead of a secondary school they found themselves outside a barracks housing Chinese or Soviet advisors to the NVA, hundreds of whom Simons and his men killed within minutes of touching down, not only making them 'good Communists' but preventing them from reinforcing the Son Tay guards. Within ten minutes Simons had mopped up and had his men re-embarked and lifted to the Son Tay compound where they helped the assault and security elements eliminate dozens of guards at the prison.

A pair of students at MACV Recondo School remain alert while waiting for exfiltration after a three day operation on Hon Tri Island in the Bay of Nha Trang. Such operations were a standard part of Recondo training and often resulted in enemy contacts. (US Army)

Despite the smoothness of the assault, however, the raiders discovered that there were no POWs. They had been moved elsewhere. Less than thirty minutes after the raid began, the raiders were back in their choppers and heading back to Thailand. Only one raider had been wounded and he only slightly. The raid had gone perfectly, even Simon's landing at the wrong complex having proven fortuitous. However, the whole reason for the raid had been to free POWs, and there were no POWs. The Son Tay Raid, despite some press reports to the contrary, was not a failure; it was a huge success. It proved graphically to the North Vietnamese that they were vulnerable to attacks on installations at home. As a result, they had to tie up thousands of troops guarding installations within North Vietnam. They also lost credibility with the Chinese. Indirectly, the raid also led to improved treatment for American POWs. It should not be forgotten, either, that Simons' party of fifty-six raiders had killed over 200 of the enemy, many of them foreign advisors, without taking a

single loss themselves. Some estimates of the number killed run much higher. The Special Forces men and the Air Force and Navy pilots supporting them had done their jobs perfectly. It was a classic raid — in suddenly, hit hard, get out fast — but the intelligence had been wrong, a failure which points up the fact that intelligence is critical to special operations, especially raids into enemy territory. Who knows what might have happened if politicians in the United States would have had the courage to use this kind of weapon to its fullest.

46th Special Forces Company (Airborne) and UITG/FANK

During the Vietnam War, Special Forces personnel were engaged in training troops for other Southeast Asian countries. Company D, 1st Special Forces Group (Airborne) arrived in Thailand in October of 1966, to train Thai troops in counterinsurgency and conventional military skills. On 15 April 1967 the 46th Special Forces Company (Airborne) was activated using personnel of Company D, 1st SFG (Abn). Among the duties of the 46th Company was training the Royal Thai Regiment for deployment to Vietnam in September of 1967. By early 1968 the 46th Special Forces Company (Abn) had an authorized strength of 369 personnel and was assigned to *Lopburi*. Its B-Detachments were at *Muang Sakon Nakhon, Pakchong*, and *Ban Kachon*. Frequently the A-Detachments were split among villages along the Northeastern border of Thailand where they helped with civic action and with anti-Communist-guerrilla activities. On 31 March 1972, HHD, 3rd Battalion, 1st SFG (Abn) was formed from the 46th Special Forces Company. This unit remained in Thailand helping prepare the Thais to defend themselves from Communist insurgencies until April of 1974.

US Army Vietnam Individual Training Group (VITG), formed of US Army Special Forces instructors, was established in South Vietnam on 1 November 1970 to train troops of the *Republique Khymer* (Cambodia). Training lasted for fifteen weeks and stressed light infantry skills. Training centers were at *Long Hai, Chi Lang, Dong Ba Thin,* and *Phuoc Tuy*. In May of 1972, this unit's designation was changed to Forces Armee Nationale Khmer (FANK). As of 30 December 1972 the unit was deactivated.

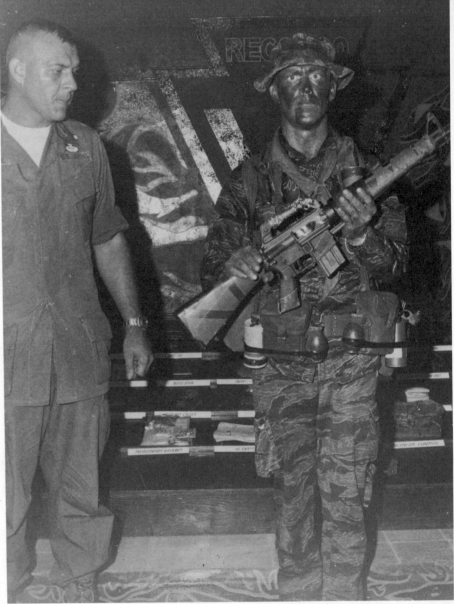

(Above) During March of 1969 a Special Forces instructor from the 5th SFG (Abn) assigned to the MACV Recondo School explains a student's equipment during a training lecture. The rifle is camouflaged and Black tape is used to keep grenades and other equipment secure and quiet.

(Left) A US advisor to the Vietnamese Hac Bao (Black Panther) Strike Company, an elite unit of the 1st ARVN Infantry Division looks over captured weapons with an Australian advisor. Note the Black beret.

LRRPs and Rangers

Shortly after the commitment of conventional ground combat units to Vietnam in 1965, division and brigade commanders realized they needed specific intelligence about their areas of operation. Normal intelligence channels were more concerned with the 'big picture' and the intelligence supplied was usually outdated. As a result, experienced combat veterans from the divisions and brigades — chosen for their skill in the bush, their alertness, their patrolling ability, and their willingness to volunteer for dangerous missions — were formed into Long Range Reconnaissance Patrols (LRRPs, pronounced *lirps*) or later LRPs (Long Range Patrols, still pronounced *lirps*). Originally created on a provisional basis, they were normally of platoon strength or less.

At first, LRRPs received no special training, but in September of 1966, the Reconnaissance/Commando (Recondo) School was established at Nha Trang, and many LRRPs were sent to this school for training. Included in the curriculum were those skills most applicable to small unit clandestine patrols in hostile territory, which included survival, field medicine, land navigation, silent movement, photography, communications, helicopter insertion and extraction, and escape and evasion.

But while tactics were being taught at the Recondo School they were also evolving in the field. Small teams — usually of four men — proved most effective. Normally, the four man team was organized with a point man, a team leader, a radioman, and a rearguard ('tailgunner'). Alertness and silence were absolute necessities for the LRRPs when on an operation since they were too few to engage in a pitched battle. LRRPs generally slept in shifts with equipment loosened, but still tight enough to move out immediately. When a team stopped, they automatically assumed defensive positions covering 360 degrees. To insure silent movement, sling swivels were removed from weapons, and equipment was taped to deaden any sound of metal or plastic. Camouflage tape was applied to weapons and equipment, and exposed skin was camouflaged. Since silence was so critical, communication when on patrol was normally through hand signals, taps on the shoulder, notes on paper (which was not discarded where the enemy might find it), or whispers directly into the ear. Radio communications were as silent as possible via pushing the radio talk button in a series of coded clicks. Aircraft flying in the vicinity monitored these calls in case emergency extraction was necessary or to relay messages.

As much as possible, LRRPs avoided contact with the enemy. Their primary job was intelligence gathering rather than combat. If LRRPs discovered an enemy unit, they often called in artillery fire, helicopter gunships, or tactical air support to destroy an enemy. Airmobile infantry might also be called in as a reaction unit once the LRRPs had located the enemy. While on patrol LRRPs kept their weapons ready in case combat could not be avoided, and if they had to fight they hit hard, fast, and first, trying to kill every enemy so that there would be none left to pursue them or to alert larger units. Occasionally, the LRRPs found themselves in a running firefight as they attempted to fight their way to a point where they could be extracted by chopper.

In very special situations LRRPs sometimes acted as the hunters rather than the hunted. When specific intelligence might be gained by 'snatching' a member of the local VC cadre, for example, LRRPs might carry out such an operation. More likely, however, they carried out hunter/killer operations in which they would set ambushes along VC trail networks. These ambushes made highly effective use of interlocking fields of fire, Claymore mines, and detonating cord in ditches along the side of the trail to catch any VC who dived for cover. Many LRRPs were trained as snipers and would eliminate enemy troops from a distance and then fade back into the bush.

The LRRPs' weapons reflected their need for firepower and compactness. The XM177E2 short version of the M-16 rifle was probably the most popular weapon, though standard M-16s and M-16s equipped with the M203 40MM grenade launcher also saw wide usage. Less commonly encountered were the M2 .30 caliber Carbine, M3 'Grease Gun', or 12 gauge Ithaca or Remington shotgun. The shotgun would normally be used by a pointman for rapidly clearing a trail should he encounter the enemy at close range. Occasional-

During the mid-1960s two US Ranger advisors to the Vietnamese Rangers, the *Biet Dong Quan* (BDQ) take part in a briefing. (US Army)

During the mid-1960s a US advisor to the Vietnamese Rangers observes hand-to-hand combat training. The advisor wears the Maroon beret of the Rangers and a Ranger pocket patch on his right breast pocket. At this time quite a bit of leeway was allowed in personal weapons, hence the Colt or Smith & Wesson magnum revolver on his hip. (US Army)

ly the AK-47 was used, however most LRRPs avoided it because of its distinctive sound which would immediately draw fire from any US troops in the vicinity. However, when operating in enemy territory where ammo resupply might be difficult, the AK-47 was occasionally chosen. Whatever weapon they chose LRRPs would carry as much ammo as possible. As many as thirty magazines might be carried in bandoliers and pouches. Additional weapons included various sidearms and a good supply of grenades — M26A1s, M34 'Willie Petes', and M18 'smokes'. Claymore mines were carried for use in protecting LRRPs at night, or when setting ambushes, though LRRPs also liked the Claymore because it was a ready source of C4 explosives, useful for everything from boobytraps to rapidly heating rations.

Since they operated in enemy controlled territory, rations and water were also problems for LRRPs. Eventually, special freeze-dried LRRP rations were developed, but they took a great deal of water. As a result a trademark of the LRRP — along with a lot of ammo — was a lot of canteens. In the early part of the war LRRPs generally wore the standard Green jungle utilities sometimes dyed black. Tiger stripe camouflage utilities were popular when they could be obtained in American sizes. Some LRRPs made their own by painting stripes on green utilities. While a Black beret was occasionally worn by the LRRPs, it was rarely seen on operations. Flop or 'boonie' hats were worn, or just an OD scarf or towel was used as a head cover. Special 'boonie' hats with a large Orange dot on the interior were used by LRRPs and other special operations troops so that the Orange part could be turned out to help a chopper pilot spot them for extraction. Many LRRPs also wore pieces of NVA/VC equipment so their profile would not be obviously American if spotted along a trail.

By late 1967 the Long Range Reconnaissance Patrols (LRRPs) were known as Long Range Patrols (LRPs) and had become more formalized in their organization. Each division now had a LRP company assigned as follows:

1st Air Cav	Company E,	52nd Infantry	(LRP)
1st Infantry Division	Company F,	52nd Infantry	(LRP)
4th Infantry Division	Company E,	20th Infantry	(LRP)
	Company E,	58th Infantry	(LRP)
9th Infantry Division	Company E,	50th Infantry	(LRP)
23rd Infantry Division	Company E,	51st Infantry	(LRP)
25th Infantry Division	Company F,	50th Infantry	(LRP)
101st Airborne Division	Company F,	58th Infantry	(LRP)

The 199th Infantry Brigade (Light) also had Company F, 51st Infantry (LRP) assigned. The 11th Infantry Brigade and the 173rd Airborne Brigade each had a smaller sixty-one man detachment. US Army Vietnam had two of these smaller detachments assigned as well, while HQ of 2nd Field Force had Company D, 151st Infantry (LRP) assigned directly to it. This last unit was an Indiana National Guard unit which had volunteered for service in Vietnam.

As of 1 January 1969, the 75th Infantry, which traced its lineage to the World War II deep penetration unit, Merrill's Marauders, was reactivated as the parent unit of all LRP companies, now designated as Ranger infantry companies. However, since the Ranger Department wanted to maintain the high standards associated with the term 'Ranger', it was stipulated, that only those men who had completed Ranger training could wear the Ranger arc.

Each of these new Ranger companies was standardized at a strength of 118 men (three officers and 115 enlisted). It was organized into a company HQ of one officer and seventeen enlisted men, and two fifty man platoons. The basic element of each platoon was a six man patrol. These Ranger companies assigned to brigades were normally only half-companies of sixty men. Ranger companies were assigned as follows:

1st Air Cav	Company H,	75th Infantry	(Ranger)
1st Infantry Division	Company I,	75th Infantry	(Ranger)
4th Infantry Division	Company K,	75th Infantry	(Ranger)
1st Brigade, 5th Infantry Division (Mechanized)	Company P,	75th Infantry	(Ranger)
9th Infantry Division	Company E,	75th Infantry	(Ranger)
23rd Infantry Division	Company G,	75th Infantry	(Ranger)
25th Infantry Division	Company F,	75th Infantry	(Ranger)
3rd Brigade, 82nd Airborne Division	Company O,	75th Infantry	(Ranger)
101st Airborne Division	Company L,	75th Infantry	(Ranger)
173rd Airborne Brigade	Company N,	75th Infantry	(Ranger)
199th Infantry Brigade (Light)	Company M,	75th Infantry	(Ranger)
I Field Force	Company C,	75th Infantry	(Ranger)
II Field Force	Company D,	75th Infantry	(Ranger)

US Ranger advisor to the BDQ wears the well-known Viet Ranger helmet cover and leaf pattern utilities. (Don Valentine)

In addition to carrying out the long range patrol mission, Rangers also served as the brigade or divisional reaction force and often supplied personnel for special missions.

Many other Rangers served in Vietnam. Graduates of Ranger training were spread throughout units in Vietnam where their knowledge of jungle survival techniques and patrolling proved invaluable. Approximately 2,000 Rangers also acted as advisors to the Vietnamese Rangers — the Biet Dong Quan. US Rangers had helped establish the Vietnamese ranger training centers at Trung Lap, Tet Son, and Duc My, and continued to serve in the field with BDQ battalions. By the end of the war, almost 300 US Rangers had been either killed in action or were missing in action.

While the contributions of LRRPs and Rangers in Vietnam did not receive the publicity which accompanied those of the Special Forces, their value was incalculable.

During July of 1968 a LRRP from the 9th Infantry Division checks his URC-10 emergency radio, which was widely used by Special Forces, LRRPs, and Rangers. He wears slant pocket jungle utilities and the Black beret sometimes seen on LRRPs in Vietnam. The MACV Recondo School pocket patch on his left pocket indicates his graduation from the Recondo training course. (US Army)

During May of 1970 a LRRP of Company D (Ranger), 75th Infantry assigned to II Field Force acts as point man for his patrol. (US Army)

(Above Right) In May of 1970, members of the Long Range Patrol from Company D (Ranger), 75th Infantry report to their team leader after a reconnaissance of the area. An Olive Drab scarf is worn as a sweatband by the LRP on the left. Sweatbands were widely worn by LRRPs and anyone else carrying out long range patrol missions. (US Army)

Browning 9mm Mk 1 Pistol
Carried by MACV/SOG Recon Teams

**75th Infantry (Ranger)
Beret Flash**

(Right) A LRRP of Company D (Ranger), 75th Infantry prepares to detonate a Claymore mine in response to movement he has heard along a trail. The fact that he is armed with the M-79 grenade launcher is a bit unusual since LRRPs were normally armed with a M-16 mounting a M203 grenade launcher, however, most LRRPs were allowed to exercise a good bit of leeway in armament selection. (US Army)

SEALS

The Navy's SEALs were formed in 1962 after the Vietnam conflict was already attracting the attention of the US armed forces. Trained to operate in all three mediums, Sea, Air, and Land — from which they took their name. The SEALs were the Navy's counterinsurgency and special warfare experts. To help counter the strong VC presence in the Mekong Delta and to supply combat swimmers to MACV/SOG and other operations the first SEAL detachments were deployed to Vietnam in 1966.

Each SEAL Team consisted of a little under 200 men with the primary tactical unit being a three man fire element. Both SEAL Team One and SEAL Team Two would see service in Vietnam. One of the first missions assigned to the SEALs was setting up observation and listening posts along suspected VC infiltration routes on the waterways and trails crisscrossing the Mekong Delta. After identifying routes and bases SEALs mounted raids to ambush the VC and destroy their bases. These reconnaissance missions proved immediately successful and their number was expanded, some observation teams staying in place for a week at a time.

SEAL patrols ranged widely on hunter-killer missions, especially in the Rung Sat Special Zone south of Saigon. Three man SEAL teams were inserted in the swampy areas of the Rung Sat by means of 'Mike' boats, and would then walk and/or swim to a point where they could possibly observe the VC, and if the opportunity arose ambush them. On such operations, SEALs usually maintained complete silence. Relying instead on operational experience together and supplemented by hand signals when needed, SEALs moved silent and deadly through the Delta. Using Claymore mines and demo cord, the SEALs would often lay booby-traps along VC trails. A variation of this technique was to set an ambush and to booby trap any likely escape routes from the killing zone.

Later in the war 'Boston Whalers' were used to insert SEAL teams. These 16 foot fiberglass boats had a very shallow draft and were well suited for operations in the Delta. The IBS (Inflatable Boat, Small) was also available, though it was used more often for clandestine insertions from submarines along the North Vietnamese coast. Whatever type of craft was used for the insertion, as soon as the SEALs were dropped off, the boat would immediately move downstream so the position of the team was not compromised. SEALs were also inserted by the choppers of Naval Light Helicopter Attack Squadrons. In some cases SEALs dove directly into the water from the chopper, then swimming to their objective.

In 1966 the SEALs, as well as the Army's Special Forces, had become involved in the ICEX (Intelligence and Exploitation) program which was aimed at identifying and neutralizing the VC infrastructure within South Vietnam. Working both with ICEX and independently, SEALs killed or captured numerous VC, unearthed arms and supply caches, and acted as spearheads or scouts for South Vietnamese or American units operating in the Delta. SEALs assigned to MACV/SOG were used for missions into Haiphong Harbor and other points inside of North Vietnam, and as the war intensified, critical bridges along supply routes in North Vietnam were often targeted for SEAL demolition raids as well.

By 1967, as a result of the success of the SEALs in the Delta region, their numbers in-country were increased substantially. Their major base was at *Nha Be*, and SEALs maintained mobile bases on barges on the waterways of the Delta. From these mobile bases SEALs mounted hunter-killer and intelligence missions throughout the region. Occasionally SEALs were called upon to act as underwater demolition specialists when it was necessary to clear the waterways. When large scale Riverine operations were mounted SEALs frequently acted as scouts. Two good examples are CRIMSON TIDE in September of 1967, and BOLD DRAGON III in March of 1968. In addition to acting as scouts during these OPERATIONS the SEALs also blew up a number of enemy installations. During BOLD DRAGON III SEALs hit *Tanh Dinh* Island especially hard, blowing up numerous VC bunkers and destroying a VC weapons factory. In OPERATION CHARLESTON SEALs acted on intelligence from captured VC documents to hit VC wells and supply sources in the Rung Sat Special Zone.

Navy SEALs practice helicopter insertions by rapelling to the beach at their base at Nha Be during January of 1967. (US Navy)

A landing craft crew awaits the return of a SEAL team they have placed ashore during OPERATION CRIMSON TIDE on the Bassac River in the Mekong Delta during September of 1967. (US Navy)

Late in 1967 the Phoenix Program was initiated as a successor to ICEX. A key element in the Phoenix Program was the PRUs (pronounced *Prews*) — the Provincial Reconnaissance Units — elite professional strike forces drawn from local MIKE Forces and the *Chieu Hoi* (Communist turncoats), and other sources. Along with Army Special Forces, SEALs acted as advisors to the PRUs. Working as the Phoenix Program's 'direct action' arm, the PRUs operated in ten to twenty man teams under Special Forces or SEAL advisors carrying out reconnaissance, intelligence, ambush, 'snatch', or assassination missions against VC political cadre, tax collectors, or sympathizers. Due to the training and assistance provided by SEALs and other US advisors, the Phoenix Program was especially effective in the Mekong Delta.

SEALs also acted as advisors and trainers to their Vietnamese counterparts — the *Lin Dei Nugel Nghai* (LLDN). Working alongside the LLDN, SEALs coordinated many joint operations, including raids on small VC POW compounds in the Delta. On 22 November 1970, fifteen SEALs and nineteen Vietnamese successfully attacked such a VC camp.

SEALs were also assigned special security duties around US port facilities including patrols to prevent the infiltration of enemy swimmers. At Cam Ranh Bay SEALs worked with attack-trained dolphins to thwart enemy attacks on US shipping.

To carry out their special missions SEALs were equipped with a lot of special hardware unique to themselves. Their armory included the 5.56MM Stoner M63A1 light machine gun, the Ithaca M37 12 gauge shotgun, the H&K G3 assault rifle, and the 9MM Smith & Wesson Mark 22 Model O silenced pistol. Known as the 'Hush Puppy' Mark 22 had been developed for eliminating enemy sentry dogs. In Vietnam the Mark 22 also was used for silently eliminating VC or NVA. The SEALs were also equipped with more standard arms such as the M60 GPMG (in some cases cut down, lightened versions), M16, and XM177E2 rifles. A typical SEAL three man fire element would be armed with an Ithaca Model 37, an M-16 with M203 40MM grenade launcher attached, and an M63A1.

It is generally stated that the SEALs had been withdrawn from Vietnam by late 1971 or early 1972, but there are indications that at least a few SEALs were in-country and involved in special operations after these dates. During the war SEALs accounted for 580 confirmed kills and over 300 probable kills. These numbers are, no doubt, low since MACV/SOG and Phoenix 'kills' attributable to the SEALs aren't likely to have been counted. Because of their ability to attack so suddenly and silently and with such ferocity, SEALs were certainly among the US troops most feared by the VC and NVA. And that fear was well founded.

Smith & Wesson Military Mark 22 Model 0 9mm "Hush Puppy" Pistol

During September of 1967 SEALs return to base after OPERATION CRIMSON TIDE. M-60 GPMGs are mounted on each side of the boat. The round object on the left side of each of the M-60s is a tin can which was used to guide the ammunition belt more reliably. (US Navy)

(Below) SEAL laying down suppressing fire along the shore as the 'Mike' boat in which he is riding heads back to their base at *Nha Be*. His 'boonie' hat is worn over a helmet and he is wearing a flak jacket. While carrying out operations ashore SEALs would usually dispense with the helmet and jacket. (US Navy)

During September of 1967 a SEAL waits in ambush during a hunter-killer mission in the Mekong Delta. The camouflage, which includes the distinctive SEAL face camouflage is obviously effective. The camouflage beret worn by this SEAL was widely worn by SEALs. In this case the beret is flopped over the left eye in the French/Vietnamese style rather than over the right eye in US style. (US Navy)

In September of 1967 a group of SEALs are being debriefed aboard a river patrol boat after a mission. Camo berets are worn by the two SEALs in the foreground. (US Navy)

During OPERATION CRIMSON TIDE in September of 1967 Navy SEALs destroy enemy fortifications along the Bassac River. (US Navy)

As their Mike Boat departs the SEALs watch the VC fortification they have just blown up burn during CRIMSON TIDE. September 1967 (US Navy)

In September of 1967 during a mission in the Mekong Delta a SEAL returns to his landing craft with a captured VC suspect. (US Navy)

Firing an M60 GPMG from the hip a SEAL lays down suppressive fire against the shoreline during extraction after a mission. (US Navy)

(Above) SEALs checking out their gas masks prior to OPERATION PLAQUES MINE. All are wearing tiger striped utilities and the SEAL on the right is wearing a dive watch. (US Navy)

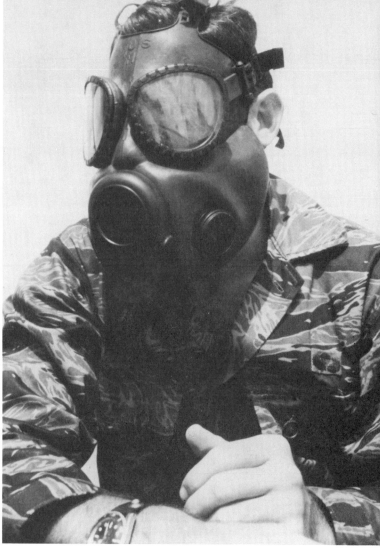

(Above) During November of 1967 a member of SEAL Team One wearing a gas mask during rehearsals for OPERATION PLAQUES MINE in November of 1967. (US Navy)

(Left) Members of SEAL Team One climb aboard a craft of the Mobile Riverine Force after a mission in November of 1967. (US Navy)

A tired member of SEAL Team One after a mission during November of 1967. He is wearing a camouflaged beret and scarf. (US Navy)

(Above Right) During November of 1967 two Navy Gunners stand by a 57MM recoilless rifle in support of SEAL operations ashore. A telescopic sight has been rigged to their weapon. (US Navy)

(Right) During November of 1967 members of SEAL Team One move down the Bassac River in an assault boat. (US Navy)

SEAL Lt (jg) removes his 'boonie' hat after he is picked up following a mission along the Bassac River during November of 1967. (US Navy)

During January of 1968 a member of SEAL Team One undergoes tactical training in the desert of Southern California. He wears the leaf pattern camouflage which became available to elite units in Vietnam during 1968. (US Navy)

Seal Ammunition Carry Coats

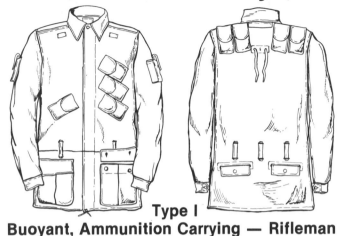

Type I
Buoyant, Ammunition Carrying — Rifleman

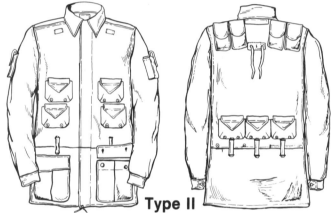

Type II
Buoyant, Ammunition Carrying — Grenadier

Type III
Buoyant, Ammunition Carrying — Radioman

In March of 1968 a SEAL sets demolition charges to destroy a VC bunker on Tanh Dinh Island during operation BOLD DRAGON III. A flak jacket is worn over his tiger stripes. (US Navy)

Members of a SEAL team check their weapons prior to insertion. Of special interest are the H&K G3 rifle carried by the SEAL the upper right and the grenadier's vest for 40mm grenades worn by the SEAL at the lower right. October 1968 (US Navy)

During March of 1968 SEALs are being extracted under VC fire after blowing up enemy bunkers on Tanh Dinh Island as part of BOLD DRAGON III. The man on the right is providing cover fire with an M-79 grenade launcher. (US Navy)

SEALs man their weapons as they prepare to be inserted for a mission. (US Navy)

In April of 1968 a SEAL jumps ashore from a Boston Whaler in the Rung Sat Special Zone. (US Navy)

During October of 1968 a group of SEALs aboard a Riverine craft prepare to be inserted. The SEAL in the center wears the Distinctive face camouflage patterns used by SEALs and carries additional M63A1 ammunition. (US Navy)

A SEAL crouches behind cover during a training operation. A 40mm grenade launcher is mounted below the barrel of the M-16. (US Navy)

Stoner M63A1

(Above) SEALs disembarking during a mission on Tanh Dinh Island in March of 1968. Already ashore are ARVN troops taking part in the mission. The lead SEAL in the water carries an M63A1 with a 150 round drum magazine. (US Navy)

(Above Right) SEAL Team being inserted for a mission via helicopter. (US Navy)

US Navy Underwater Knife

Blade is 7 1/4 inches long with saw teeth on the back edge. All metal parts are made of a non-magnetic, stain resistant, non-ferrous alloy. Sheath is made of a gray fiber glass.

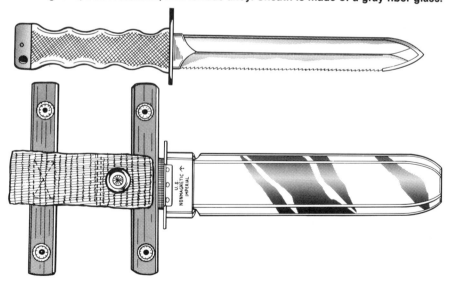

(Right) Navy Armored Troop Carrier of the type used by Riverine forces and which sometimes were used to insert SEALs passes under a fortified bridge on the *Bay Hap River* during April of 1970. (US Navy)

US Marine Corps Recons

Marine Recons are considered an elite among a force that already considers itself to be an elite force. Trained in airborne, helicopter, SCUBA, and small boat insertions; communications, long range patrolling, intelligence gathering, and other special operations skills; the Recons perform missions similar to the Army's LRRPs or Special Forces, and the Navy SEALs. While primarily an intelligence gathering unit, in Vietnam the Recons were used as raiders and advisors to CIDG units as well. Normally, divisional reconnaissance battalions were charged with missions in support of the divisions to which they were assigned, while Force Recon companies were assigned to pre-assault and post-assault reconnaissance in support of landing forces. Force Recons are believed to have been used along the North Vietnam coast line to evaluate possible sites for amphibious landings.

Marine Recons of the 1st Force Reconnaissance Company were among the earliest US combat troops in Vietnam when they carried out beach reconnaissance missions before the landing of the 9th Marine Expeditionary Brigade in March of 1965. During a later beach reconnaissance mission the 1st Force Recon Company took its first casualty when one of its men was killed in a clash with the VC.

Although 'deep reconnaissance' platoons of Marine Recon units can carry out missions up to 100 kilometers ahead of the unit to which they are assigned, in Vietnam most reconnaissance missions were carried out much closer to major units. During the early part of the Marine commitment, most Recon patrols consisted of twelve to twenty-four men, though later in the war smaller LRRP size units of four to six men were found to be more effective. A major limiting factor on the length of time that these early patrols could stay out was the short battery life and short range of the PRC-10 radio. Only a limited number of batteries, which died quickly in Vietnam, could be carried, but with the introduction of the PRC-25 with longer lasting batteries the length of patrols was increased by 1966.

During 1965 the 3rd Recon Battalion and 1st Force Recon Company arrived in-country, followed in 1966 by the 1st Recon Battalion, and in 1967 by the 3rd Force Recon Company. As of October 1965 the 1st Force Recon Company had a strength of nine officers and 103 enlisted men and was assigned to the 3rd Recon Battalion.

Late in 1965 the 2nd Platoon, 1st Force Recon Company was assigned to the Special Forces camp at *Ba To* and the 3rd Platoon, 1st Force Recon Company was assigned to the Special Forces camp at *Tra Bang*. Both platoons were to be used on 'Bird Watcher' deep penetration missions. Eventually Recons would operate in Laos and North Vietnam. Marine Recons were also assigned to MACV/SOG for cross border operations. An indication of the toughness of the Recons can be gained from the experience of one Recon Marine assigned to 'Bird Watcher' missions out of *Ba To*. Wounded and captured by the NVA, he escaped twice, the second time by forcing two NVA soldiers at knife point to carry him back to *Ba To*!

Recons were used for various other types of missions as well. In operations such as BLACK FERRET in November of 1965, for example, two platoons of the 1st Recon Battalion acted as screening units. Other Recons served as advisors to the CIDG in I Corps, and still others acted as quick response patrols providing security for downed Marine helicopters until they could be lifted out for salvage or repairs. While some of their assigned missions misused the Recons, who were intended for intelligence gathering, the Recons carried them out well. During 1965 Recon companies had the highest VC kill rate of any unit in-country. A more effective use of the Recon units was in 'Stingray' missions during which the Recons would locate enemy concentrations and call in air or artillery strikes. Recons were especially useful for patrols along the DMZ and in the hilly area north of *Hue* near the DMZ. It should be noted that Recon patrols often went north of the DMZ.

Throughout the siege of *Khe Sanh*, Recon units including Company B, 3rd Battalion, and 3rd Platoon, Company D, 3rd Recon Battalion were present, but they were used in reserve rather than as reconnaissance troops. Other Recon troops were used to deter-

During the fall of 1965 members of the 3rd Recon Battalion cross the Mong River during a sweep and clear mission. All are wearing standard USMC fatigue caps. (USMC)

mine NVA and VC strength, and to locate concentrations in other areas of I Corps, especially around *Hue* during the Tet Offensive, to which the Siege of *Khe Sanh* was a corollary. Recons were also involved in scouting and recon missions for other large-scale Marine operations. Elements of the 3rd Recon Battalion were used extensively in OPERATIONS KENTUCKY and SCOTLAND during 1968 and 1969 respectively.

The 3rd Recon Battalion left Vietnam during November of 1969, along with the 3rd Marine Division, and was followed in August of 1970 by the 3rd Force Recon Company. The 1st Recon Battalion left in March of 1971 with the 1st Marine Division, and was followed the next month by the 1st Force Recon Company. Recons had been assigned to MACV/SOG, especially CCN and the 'Maritime Studies Group' and a few may have stayed around with SOG until 1972 or later.

(Left) A USMC Recon wearing SCUBA gear for an underwater infiltration mission. Mid-1960 (USMC)

(Right) Two USMC Recons observe an enemy position while on a reconnaissance mission during the mid-1960s. Camouflage helmet covers are being worn as head gear. The Recon at the right carries a M3A1 SMG. (USMC)

USMC Recon Wings

(Below) USMC Recons on patrol near the Laotian border and the DMZ during 1967. They are wearing the ever popular 'boonie' hats and are heavily-laden for an extended patrol. (USMC)

Airforce Combat Control Teams And Combat Security Police

The Air Force had two units serving in Vietnam which should be classified as 'special forces' — the Combat Control Teams (CCTs) and the Combat Security Police (CSPs). And while the elite PJs of the Aerospace Rescue and Recovery Service were as much an elite unit as the CCTs or CSPs, the PJs' mission was to rescue downed airmen, and while this task often included missions behind enemy lines, it was not a 'special forces' mission within the parameters of this book.

Combat Control Teams

During the Vietnam War, the CCTs received their initial training at Sewart AFB, Arkansas. In addition to being trained as air traffic controllers and as parachutists, CCTs were also trained in communications, emergency first aid, patrol, ambush, and counter-ambush tactics, the establishment of drop zones and landing zones, and helicopter insertions and extractions. Combat Control Teams received more intensive weapons training than any other Air Force unit except the Combat Security Police.

CCTs assigned to aerial port detachments worked closely with the Army's Special Forces at Special Forces camps where the CCTs would guide transport aircraft to either land on the camp airstrip or drop supplies. CCTs also acted as pathfinders for airborne operations. In some situations CCTs called in air strikes to support Special Forces camps. It's believed that CCTs were used on clandestine missions along the Ho Chi Minh Trail and elsewhere to spot for USAF gunships such as 'Puff' or 'Spectre'. During the so-called siege at *Khe Sanh* CCTs marked drop zones or landing zones and also stood by to assume control of incoming C-123s and C-130s should the Marine control tower at *Khe Sanh* have lost radio contact.

Within South Vietnam CCTs originally came under the control of the Airlift Control Center (ALCC) at Tan Son Nhut, but after its activation in October of 1966, Combat Control Teams became part of the 834th Air Division. Individual Combat Control Teams were assigned to the three aerial port squadrons or the smaller aerial port detachments within the 834th Air Division.

In addition to their contribution to the defense of *Khe Sanh*, CCTs also played an important role in aerial supply efforts during the Tet Offensive, operations in Cambodia and Laos, and the 1972 Easter Invasion. These major operations, however, were only among the more visible CCT missions. Throughout the war in Southeast Asia at small airstrips at Special Forces 'fighting camps' all over Vietnam CCTs made sure that critical supplies made it through the pipeline.

Combat Security Police

The Air Force's other special operations unit came into existence as a result of VC attacks against US air bases. The Combat Security Police (CSP) were trained as Air Force 'Rangers' and were equipped to function as a quick reaction force should an air base come under attack, or as a seek and destroy unit which could set ambushes to destroy enemy infiltrators outside or on the perimeter of a base.

The forerunner of the Combat Security Police was the 1041st Security Police Squadron which received sixteen weeks of Ranger type training from Army Ranger instructors at Schofield Barracks, Hawaii as part of 'OPERATION SAFESIDE.

As a result of the success of the 1041st Security Police Squadron during its tour in Vietnam, Combat Security Police Squadrons were formed and trained as an elite light infantry, combining the skills of the Army's Rangers and the British RAF Regiment. Each CSP

During August of 1968 members of the USAF 821st Combat Security Police (CSP) Squadron man a .50 caliber machine gun at Phan Rang Air Base. All are wearing the 'boonie' hat and camouflage utilities. (USAF)

squadron had an authorized strength of twenty-one officers and 538 enlisted men. The squadron was broken into three flights, each with six officers and 161 enlisted men. Each of these flights consisted of three field sections of one officer and thirty-two enlisted men and one support section of one officer and sixty-three enlisted men. These sections were broken into ten man fire teams. Between April of 1968 and February of 1971 three Combat Security Police Squadrons — the 821st, 822nd, and 823rd — served in Vietnam. Although each squadron was nominally assigned to Phan Rang Air Base during its tour in Vietnam, flights or even sections of the Combat Security Police Squadron were often sent elsewhere on special assignment.

During March of 1968 CCTs of the 8th Aerial Port Squadron prepare to use smoke grenades to signal transport aircraft the location of the drop zone for supplies at Khe Sanh. At Khe Sanh these CCTs wear the extra protection of helmets and flak jackets. (USAF)

USAF Combat Control Team Beret Badge
(Post Vietnam)

(Left) Two members of the 8th Aerial Port Squadron Combat Control Team (CCT) maintain radio contact with USAF transport aircraft delivering supplies to the Special Forces camp at *Cai Cai* during April of 1968. During the Vietnam War CCTs did not have a beret badge so they wore parachutist's wings on their Dark Blue berets. (USAF)

In October of 1969 CCTs help a C-130 Hercules take off from a landing strip. (USAF)

A CCT at Cai Cai Special Forces Camp directs in a C-130 delivering supplies to the camp.
April 1968 (USAF)